# Raising Responsible, Emotionally Mature Children

"Perplexed parents will find a wealth of useful—even transformative—information in this wise book. The principles described by Dr. Allen can improve all relationships, not just parent/child."
**Carroll Morris, MA, CH, MRET and author of *The Complete Caregiver Support Guide***

"I thoroughly enjoyed your book. I would recommend this book to parents who have kids of all ages and to therapists. I found myself immediately using many of your techniques with my teens and found that instead of yelling, we were able to talk."
**Laura Gomez Weakley**
**Licensed Professional Counselor**

"Finally, a book with the perfect blend of principles, knowledge, and real-life examples that effectively teach us how to become the parents our children deserve and need. My absolute favorite go-to parenting resource."
**Keri Krout**
**Mother of seven, parent coach, early childhood educator**

"This book will teach you how to make your home a safe and nurturing place—where children and parents are allies in the important work of building self esteem and learning how to deal with challenges.  I know because I used these principle-based skills as young mother and a junior high school teacher. Now they are invaluable when resolving conflicts with my grandchildren.  The results continue to amaze me."
**Janis Blake**
**Mother, grandmother, and former school teacher**

"When I was young, I had no idea my parents were using the skills taught in this book.  What I did know was that they took time to listen and talk with me. As a result, we developed trust and I learned to take responsibility for my choices.  And now that I'm a mother I use the skills every day.  I love them! I am able to create teachable moments and a more peaceful environment."
**Vallarie Blake Nuttall**
**Mother of six**

"As one who works daily with college students, I can say that this book is a compelling look at modern parenting with a practical approach to real-life situations. The methods will greatly assist parents in developing ways to improve raising their children. Dr. Allen has the insight and experience from which any and all parents can benefit."

**Jonathan Morrell, Director**
**Student Support Services**
**Dixie State University**

# Raising Responsible, Emotionally Mature Children

*Roger K. Allen, Ph.D.*

 Leadership Press

ISBN: 9780979783142

PRINTED IN USA
ISBN: 0979783143
Library of Congress Control Number: 2015902474
Leadership Press, Littleton, CO

To our children:

Melinda
Jonathan
Cheryl-Lynn
Cristina

# Acknowledgments

IN COUNTLESS WAYS, WE BUILD upon the ideas, labor, and love of those who have come before us. It would be impossible for me to give adequate credit to all who have not only made it possible for me to write this book, but whose ideas have influenced my thoughts about parenting.

Certainly one person who stands out for me is my father, the late C. Kay Allen. So much of what I've learned about human relations, in general, and the parenting skills which I teach in this book, build upon his work. A true renaissance man and successful businessman throughout most of his career, he founded the Human Values Institute in the early 1970s in order to disseminate principles of human behavior. His two books, *Journey from Fear to Love* (1976) and *The Ways and Power of Love* (1992), express his deep insight into people and relationships. Although this work was an avocation rather than career, it was his highest "calling." As a popular speaker and teacher, he touched the lives of hundreds of thousands of people. This book develops and expands upon principles I learned from him.

I also want to acknowledge my family. My wife, Judy Bickmore Allen, has not only offered tremendous support throughout my career and as I've worked on this book, but also was the primary caregiver of our children. I learned from her by watching her parent. She loved our children dearly and taught them responsibility from an early age. She was and is a wise parent.

I'm also grateful for our three children, Melinda Otting, Jonathan Allen, and Cheryl-Lynn Adams, and our "adopted" daughter and exchange student, Cristina Kramp, from Ecuador. I deeply love each of them as well as their spouses and children. When in the younger child-rearing years, I didn't think much about what it would be like to be a grandfather of a large family. But I have to say I feel the same love for my children's children as I do for each of them. They have brought much joy into our lives.

I was much younger and, of course, immature when I began parenting. I was little prepared for this awesome responsibility and so learned from real-life experiences as we went along. My kids grew up. I also grew up, thanks to them. Looking back, I have to say that we had wonderful and sometimes challenging experiences. And the best news is that these relationships continue. I cherish my relationship with my adult children and continue to learn from them as we talk and as I watch how they live and parent.

There are certainly many professionals who have contributed to this book. I've read many books on parenting, particularly the last few years, as I've thought about this book and formalized the framework, principles, and skills you'll read as you go through these pages.

I'm grateful to many parents and public school teachers whom I've taught, allowing me to refine these ideas. Two teachers come to mind. Janis Blake and Deanna Mecham embraced the ideas and used them to change not only their own classrooms but an entire school. They were a successful laboratory for these principles in the early days of my teaching and I appreciate the commitment and even courage which they demonstrated as they applied these skills with their students, sometimes in the face of great opposition.

As always, I'm thankful to my colleagues at the Human Development Institute for their collaboration and support. I could not have found a better business associate in the early days of HDI than Randy Hardman. I also appreciate the support from so many of the early staff, Vera Spencer, Joan Hall, Ingrid Bertussi, Blaine and Katherine Porter, and too many others to name. In more recent years, I'm grateful for support from Steve Churchill, who has been a friend and important sounding board and fount of wisdom as I've thought through the direction of HDI. And, most recently, I'm grateful for the insight and support of Justin Riggs, a man of integrity, committed to blessing the lives of others.

Finally, I want to acknowledge the thousands of clients and participants in HDI workshops and seminars throughout so many years. I'm honored that you were willing to trust us in your journey of personal growth, and I feel blessed by your love and loyalty. So many volunteered their time to assist in classes and help share our story. As I close my eyes and look back on my career, it is your faces I see and memories of you that I will always treasure.

# Table of Contents

# Introduction

*A*S IMPORTANT AS YOUR OBLIGATIONS *as a doctor, lawyer, or business leader will be, you are a human being first, and those human connections—with spouses, with children, with friends—are the most important investments you will ever make. At the end of your life, you will never regret not having passed one more test, not winning one more verdict, or not closing one more deal. You will regret time not spent with a husband, a child, a friend, or a parent.... Our success as a society depends not on what happens inside the White House but on what happens inside your house.* (Barbara Bush, speaking to the graduating class of Wellesley College, June 1990)

I believe there is no more important work than that which goes on inside the walls of our homes. You probably agree. It is in the home where we shape the lives of our greatest legacy, our children. And yet fulfilling this awesome responsibility is not easy. Raising children requires an abundance of understanding, patience, perseverance, dedication, and emotional maturity. And that's just the first twelve months of life! Multiply this by eighteen-plus years, add in a few more children, and you have embarked on one of life's most challenging journeys.

Not only is family life chaotic, with so many emotional demands and competing priorities, but social and economic changes within society are making parenting more and more challenging all the time. The fact that we love our children and truly desire to be good parents does not make the journey easy nor guarantee an idyllic family life.

Nevertheless, I am optimistic. You are reading this book because you care about what happens inside your home. You love your children and want to give them the very best. This means that your frustrations and missteps are not due to bad intent, but rather ignorance, faulty beliefs, or a tendency to react when stress is high and you're not sure what to do. The good news is that, because of your love and positive intent, you can continue to learn and grow and become even more loving and nurturing parents.

The **purpose of this book** is to teach you a framework and set of skills to help you create a nurturing home; a home which blends the qualities of love and compassion with clear expectations and accountability. You'll learn to communicate with your children (from toddlers to teens) in ways that build safety and trust, increase their self-worth, foster emotional maturity, and instill an attitude of personal responsibility. Specifically, the book will help you:

* Establish loving authority in your home
* Create conditions that open up communication and build trust
* Build an atmosphere of harmony rather than criticism, bickering, and put-downs
* Resolve disagreements and conflicts constructively and without power struggles
* Give up parenting habits that destroy self-esteem and weaken relationships
* Teach your children to assume responsibility for their feelings and actions
* Set limits and enforce discipline without being heavy-handed

In the first few chapters, I define the goal of parenting, discuss three family climates, and share nine principles that form the foundation of a nurturing home. These chapters create a framework to guide our parenting.

Most of the book—chapters four through ten—are about the daily communication and interactions between family members. These chapters will teach you skills to communicate in ways that will strengthen your relationship with your children and help them grow into capable and responsible adults.

I'll present a communications model (the HERO principle) to guide you in all your communication, but particularly during moments of tension and conflict, when it is easy to say and do things that are harmful rather than helpful to family relationships or family members.

Most readers will go through the book from front to back. However, if you're looking for specific techniques that can help you improve your parenting today, you can go directly to the skill chapters (7-9). If you do so, I encourage you to circle back and read the other chapters, which will give you an indispensable context for fully understanding the skill chapters.

The skills are powerful. By learning and practicing them, you will improve the way you parent so you can enjoy your children more and positively influence their development.

I have been teaching these principles and skills for many years and I am pleased to make them more widely available in a book. I'm delighted that you have decided to join me on this important journey.

Let's get started.

Roger Kay Allen, Ph.D.
www.raisingresponsiblechildren.com
Littleton, Colorado
January, 2015

# CHAPTER 1

# The Goal of Parenting

ISN'T TECHNOLOGY WONDERFUL? WHEN I was a boy if I wanted to change the channel on the TV, I had to get up and go the TV. Now, all we do is point a remote in the general direction of the TV, press a button and change the channel. It is easy.

Then I began thinking how nice it would be if someone would invent a remote for our children. After all, with our life experience and wisdom, we know what is best for them if we could just get them to listen and follow our good council. How nice to have a remote in hand and send commands to our children so they immediately stop whining, clean their rooms, do their homework, accept "no" for an answer, and thank us for being such good parents.

Of course, this isn't the nature of our human experience. It fails to respect the self-responsibility or free will of our children and the fact that growth is an internal process and not something which can be imposed from without.

So, what is the goal or purpose of our parenting?

I want to give you my answer by sharing a story that goes back to when our children were very young. It was a Sunday afternoon and I'd just settled onto our bed with a book, hoping to do a little reading, maybe even nod off.

Suddenly, I heard a commotion going on down the stairs. Melinda (six at the time) was chasing Jon (four) around the circle of our living room, kitchen, and dining room. Jon was giggling as he ran, with his sister in close pursuit shouting, "Give it back."

I walked down the stairs. "What's going on?" Without a word, they both darted past me and upstairs to their rooms. Back upstairs I knelt and knocked on Jon's door. "Jon, would you come out?" I waited a moment. The door opened a crack and Jon, a sheepish little grin on his face, peered up at me. I took his hand. "Come with me." We walked down the hallway to Melinda's door. I knocked and waited. I knocked again. "Now, Melinda, I know you're in there." The door finally opened. I took her hand and gently pulled her into the hallway. "Will you guys tell me what's happening?"

As you can imagine, Melinda spoke up. "Jon took my book."

Jon quickly defended himself. "She wasn't reading it. She never lets me use her things."

I chuckled as each immediately blamed the other. Such a natural human response, a defense mechanism we all use so we can feel justified in our behavior and shift responsibility (blame) to someone else. No one wants to be found "at fault," which not only has negative connotations but so often results in punishment.

Of course this is an old pattern. We even read about it in the Bible when God asked Adam if he had eaten of the forbidden fruit. He blamed Eve. Eve blamed the serpent.

I want to suggest that it's hard to own up to our responsibility in life. Doing so requires a lot of emotional maturity, far more than I can expect from a four- and six-year-old worried about being in trouble with their dad.

But, let's pretend for a moment. If Jon were to accept responsibility, he'd say something like: "I was so bored. I've read all my books, so I thought I'd take a look at Melinda's. Besides, it's kind of fun to take her stuff and run. I get the biggest kick out of watching her get mad. Yup. I did it. I knowingly provoked her, Daddy."

If Melinda accepted responsibility, she might say, "I have plenty of books. But sometimes I like to get mad at Jon. It's fun to see him get in trouble. Besides, it feels kind of good to be the victim and have you or Mom come and rescue me."

Were our children ready to take that level of responsibility? Of course not. Most adults don't claim that much responsibility. Here we are, in our twenties, thirties, forties, or even sixties, succumbing to the tendency to make excuses, blame others, and shift responsibility from our shoulders to events, circumstances, and others.

I want to reiterate. Personal responsibility takes a lot of emotional maturity, including self-awareness, ability to manage our emotional reactions, confidence, and an ability to step outside our own skin and understand another's point of view. Lessons not easy to learn.

I wanted to interact with my children in ways that would plant seeds of responsibility even if they required time to take root and bear fruit. So, I kept talking. "What choices did you make, Jon?"

"Dad, not me, it was Melinda."

"I know, I know. It was her. But did you make any choices?"

He looked down. "I guess."

"Like what?"

"I took her book and ran."

"How do you think she felt about that?" I persisted.

"Not good."

"Yup," I said. "Is that what you wanted?" He was quiet. "What choices did you make, Melinda?"

"Dad, it wasn't me, it was Jon."

"I know. But did you make any choices?"

"I chased him and yelled at him."

I continued asking questions. "Were there other choices you each could have made? What will happen if the two of you keep fighting? Is that what you want? Jon, what can you do? Melinda, what can you do?"

We could only have this discussion because I was not in a punishing mood. I was in a good place emotionally and had not been "hooked" by the kids' little hullabaloo. In fact, it's impossible to teach responsibility if we're not living from personal responsibility.

I also need to state that I was not so much interested in solving this problem as helping my kids begin to think more deeply and develop more of a sense of ownership/responsibility for their reactions and behavior, something which is impossible in a reactive, emotional climate.

I share this story not to give you a technique but rather to offer you a different perspective. (In fact, we too often over-reason with young children.) I share it to help you see that my purpose as a parent is to help my children take responsibility or *claim ownership* of their lives.

What does that mean? Ownership of what? *Ownership of their feelings, thoughts, behavior, attitudes, choices, values, desires, decisions, relationships, grades, time, room, nutrition, etc.* You name it. This, of course, does not happen overnight. It doesn't happen from one conversation, especially with young children. It happens over time as we shift our perspective from "fixing problems" to "growing children."

As a parent, I want to interact and communicate with my children in ways that help them learn to think deeply, take ownership, solve their own problems, and make good decisions. I'm no longer imposing control from without. I'm standing at their side, loving and guiding them as they learn to navigate their way in a challenging world.

This notion changes the paradigm of parenting. It means we have to stop being responsible for our children and instead interact with them in ways that allow them to be responsible for themselves.

Perhaps the best way I can describe this is with the analogy of a flower. Have you ever watched a flower blossom? Have you ever tried to force a flower to blossom? What happens if you pull those petals apart?

What are the implications for parenting? We cannot force our children to blossom. We can only create a nurturing environment in which that can occur. We are gardeners and not mechanics.

Take a look at the chart on the next page. When a child is born, she is totally dependent upon her parents for all her needs. As she grows older, she begins to develop more autonomy and capability. By the time she's ready to leave home, we want her to be responsible and emotionally mature enough to make it on her own, to be positively self-governing. The art of parenting is guiding this process of growth into self-responsibility.

# How Responsibility Shifts Over Time

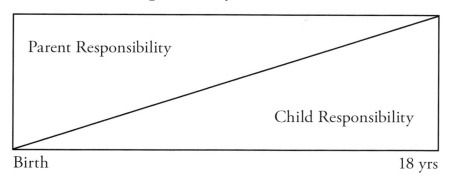

Accepting responsibility and developing emotional maturity means our children learn to:

- Know of their goodness and worth
- Feel safe enough to talk
- Delay gratification and tolerate frustration
- Act rather than react
- Solve problems and make good decisions
- Set and work toward goals
- Make and keep commitments
- Act from a moral and spiritual compass
- Respect and cooperate with others

The implications of understanding this purpose are enormous. It helps us stop reacting so we can figure out a better way to respond. It invites us to focus less on our children and more on ourselves—our thoughts, actions, and communication—and how these influence our children. It invites us to trust the natural growth and development of our children. It invites our children to think for themselves, solve their own problems, and take responsibility for their decisions. We don't click a remote to make this happen. We don't do it through force or unrighteous dominion. It is a process that occurs gradually as we focus on building loving relationships and a nurturing environment in which our children learn to take ownership of their lives.

Most of us make two mistakes in our parenting. One is we **over manage** our children by controlling, directing, lecturing, reminding, nagging, and so on. There are many ways we do this. In essence, we fail to trust our children and so we impose control from without in ways that weaken them in the long run. Second, we **overindulge** our children by sympathizing, giving in, catering, rescuing, fixing, or otherwise trying to protect them from the difficulties of life. Again, we fail to trust them to handle the difficulties and challenges of life and either neglect to set good boundaries (which would upset them) or we step in and do for them what they can learn to do for themselves. Whichever of these strategies we use, we make ourselves overly responsible and deprive our children of valuable opportunities to learn and grow.

The remainder of this book teaches principles and skills for interacting differently with our children. It will help us move from focusing on solving the immediate problem to planting the seeds of responsibility that allow them to become mature, self-governing individuals.

# CHAPTER 2

# Family Climate

HAVING CHILDREN NATURALLY INTRODUCES CHAOS into the life of a couple/parent. Not only does each new addition to the family upset the existing balance and routine of couple or family life, but children, because of their lack of development, come into the home needy, self-centered, and demanding. Add more children and pretty soon family life can seem pretty chaotic.

We deal with this chaos in one of two ways. Some parents tend to be more structured and controlling. Others tend to be more easygoing and responsive. The chart below illustrates four different family climates based on these two dimensions.

**Four Family Climates\***

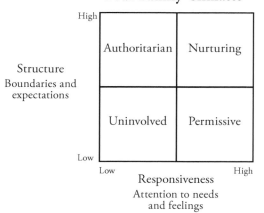

\*Diane Baumrind first proposed three types of parenting (Authoritarian, Permissive and Authoritative) in the 1960s. Maccoby and Martin built upon

Baumrind's typology by adding two dimensions: responsive and demanding and came up with four parenting types in the 1980s. Although the terms differ, somewhat, I base this model on their work.

Authoritarian parents are high on structure (clear routines, expectations, and boundaries) and low on responsiveness (not as sensitive to individual needs and feelings). Permissive parents are high on responsiveness and low on structure. Uninvolved parents are low on both dimensions. They create a climate in which there is little emotional support as well as failure to set expectations or enforce standards of conduct for their children. Finally, nurturing parents are high on both dimensions. They set expectations *and* remain emotionally responsive to their children. This is the healthiest climate and affords our children the greatest opportunity to succeed.

Eventually, we settle around a set of practices somewhere along each of these two dimensions, and this forms the climate in which we raise our children. Of course, most families are not "pure" types. There is a lot of variability in both the extent and how families express the characteristics of each of these quadrants.

The purpose of this chapter is to step back and observe our family climate so we can become more deliberate about creating a positive parenting style and the climate that will support us in raising our children. We grow as parents by becoming good at both setting expectations *and* being responsive to our children's needs and feelings. Most parents are better at one than the other. Doing both is challenging and yet the hallmark of a nurturing home. You will learn principles and communication skills, throughout this book, to do both.

I'm going to describe three of the climates—permissive, authoritarian, and nurturing—in the next few pages. I'm spending less time on the uninvolved climate because it is less common, particularly among parents who care enough about their children to read a parenting book.

## Permissive Climate (Chaos)

Permissive families are more lax. Although warm and responsive, these parents don't impose many expectations, structure, or routine on their children. Hence the children experience greater freedom and independence, such as getting their own meals, playing in the mud, or staying out late. Some parents are permissive because they dislike imposing control. They believe in individuality and allowing their children "say." Many are permissive because they are unsure of their own authority. They have trouble setting boundaries or limits. Either way, these parents tend to avoid conflict. They want their children to be happy and so may indulge them materially or emotionally. A consequence is that children have lots of power and control within these homes. And because their parents are responsive, the children may become demanding and learn to get what they want through tears, tantrums, whining, and accusations. The parents often give in to keep the peace, which only reinforces their children for acting in self-centered and demanding ways. These children may grow up to be independent, but also entitled and not as good at emotional self-regulation. They often haven't learned to do hard things and so lack discipline to stick with difficult tasks. In general, they are less likely to work hard and achieve in school or life.

**Young children example:** It is dinnertime in the McCarthy household. Martha (seven) and Beth (four) are whining and telling Mom they're bored as she tries to make dinner. Mom does her best to ignore them until she can't stand listening to them anymore. She puts on a video to keep the girls quiet and get them out of her hair. Before long, Dad is home and calls the kids to the table, but they don't want to turn off the video. He calls them three or four times and finally tells them that they can watch an extra video if they'll just come and eat their dinner. Both girls cry as they come to the table. They slump into their chairs, both in a bad mood. Mom dishes up the meal, but neither girl likes what is being served and refuses to eat. They get down a few times and wander off to the family room to try and restart the video. Dad insists they come back. They do so, crying. Dinner degenerates with Dad coaxing the girls' every bite. "Just a few more bites. Come on. Your mom went to a lot of trouble to make this nice meal." Finally, Mom can't take it any longer and gets up and prepares a hot dog and macaroni and cheese, reasoning that it's better to get something into them than have them go hungry.

**Teen example:** Mark (sixteen) was out late on Saturday night. Sunday morning his father doesn't hear him stirring and so goes to the basement door and calls down the stairs. No answer. He feels a knot in his stomach and isn't sure what to do. He goes down the stairs and knocks lightly on the door. "Mark, it's time to get ready for church." Still no answer. The father goes back upstairs and talks to his wife. They don't want the hassle of a confrontation and so decide to ignore the situation and see what Mark decides. Not surprisingly, Mark doesn't get up for church. Later in the day, Father makes the comment to Mark, "You know how bad your mom feels when you don't come with us to church. We really need you to cooperate with us, son. It affects the whole family."

Mark barks back, "I'm old enough to decide for myself, Dad. Just leave me alone."

Dad retreats, a sick feeling in his stomach.


# AN AUTHORITARIAN CLIMATE (ORDER)

This is a family climate that includes lots of structure and rules. The parents are in charge and children know what is expected of them. There are consequences (or punishment) if the children violate their parents' expectations. Generally, authoritarian parents lack sensitivity to what their children think and feel. They are insecure about their children's ability to perform or make good choices, so they either over control by putting lots of rules in place or "ride herd" over them to make sure they are doing what they're "supposed" to do. In short, parents in these families tend to over manage their children. The kids don't learn to be self-managing and so wait until they are prompted to take any kind of action. In the long run they tend to become compliant and obedient (good child) or rebellious and defiant (bad child). Unless they outright rebel, children from these families like to please and are usually well behaved. However, they are more likely to have poor social skills and suffer from depression, anxiety, or low self-esteem.

**Young children example:** It is dinnertime in the Garcia household. Mom says, "Girls, come now and set the table." Her daughters, playing in the other room, are slow to mind. "Girls, I mean NOW! If you're not here by the time I count to five, you'll go to your rooms without dinner. One…two…three… I'm telling you, get in here."

Carmen and Lucia rush around the corner, Lucia crying, "Carmen pushed me."

"I did not. You wouldn't get out of my way."

Mom: "I don't want to hear it. Now set this table." The two girls slowly set the table, bumping each other and making faces, whimpering and complaining about the other until Mom has to intervene. "Did you hear what I said? No more of this or I'll send you to your rooms."

Dad arrives home and the family sits down to eat. The girls dawdle with their food. Dad's patience is at his limit as Lucia starts to whimper. "That's it. You don't have any reason to cry. Get down from the table and go to your room right now. No dinner for you tonight."

**Teen example.** Javier was out late on Saturday night. His father doesn't hear him stirring and so goes to the top of the stairs and hollers, "Javier, time to get up. We have to leave for church in one hour." He doesn't hear his son stir, so ten minutes later he walks down the stairs and knocks, quite loudly. "Get out of that bed. It is time to get ready for church." No movement inside the room. By this time, Dad is really getting worked up. He opens the door and turns on the light. "Hey, you talk to me when I call you." Son stirs a little. "Javier, get yourself out of that bed or you'll wish you had." Father leaves the room and goes into the bathroom and pours up a glass of water to rouse his son. He returns and Javier is sitting on his bed.

"Okay, okay. Give me a break. I'm up."

Father feels victorious. "Okay. Good. I don't want to fight, but you know what day it is. You'd better be upstairs and dressed in twenty minutes."

# A Nurturing Climate (Love and Accountability)

This is a culture that includes both structure *and* responsiveness. These parents trust their own authority and use it to create a positive environment rather than over control their children. They set age-appropriate limits but also allow their children to assume responsibility by making decisions and solving problems. Family structure comes from principles and family values rather than an attempt to control the children. Rather than getting into power struggles, these parents allow consequences (natural and imposed) to operate and shape their children's behavior. The parents also feel and communicate lots of love and respect. They spend time with their kids, joining them in their world, when young, and taking time to talk and listen to them as they get older. They make positive assumptions about their children's motives and capability, allowing them to respond in a soft way, even during moments of disagreement. These children generally grow up feeling good about themselves. They show self-responsibility and are most likely to thrive in school and life.

**Young children example:** Mrs. Olsen looks at the clock and realizes that it's time to start getting dinner. She walks to the refrigerator and takes a look at the chore chart. "Okay, guys, we've got a half hour until dinner." She goes to work preparing the meal. Sally (eight) and Jared (six) keep playing in the other room. After fifteen minutes, Mom walks into the playroom. "I've got a feeling someone may be going hungry tonight. Dad will be home and we're eating in about fifteen minutes." Letting out an "Argh," Jared jumps up and goes to the kitchen to set the table. Dad arrives and the family sits down together. Sally looks at her meal and grimaces. "Yuck. I hate fish. Why don't we ever have something decent for dinner."

Dad looks up. "You don't have to eat it. It's up to you."

Sally picks at her food, eats a slice of bread and a few bites of mashed potato. In a few minutes Mom gets up and prepares three slices of apple pie. Sally whimpers when she doesn't get a slice. "Your choice," says Mom.

**Teen example:** Peter was out late on Saturday night. Sunday morning, his father doesn't hear any movement downstairs. Normally, Peter gets himself out of bed, but his father is concerned and so walks down the stairs and stands outside the door. He taps. There's no answer. He opens it a crack and looks in. "Peter, it's 7:30. We have to leave for church in an hour." He stands quietly in the doorway for a moment.

Peter rolls over.

"Dad, I'm so tired. Do I have to go today? I got home so late last night."

Dad walks over to the bed and sits on it. "I noticed you were late. In fact, I was a little worried. How did things go?"

"Okay. We just got talking and I let the time get away from me, that's all." Pause. "But I'd rather not go to church today, just this once."

Dad reaches out and puts his hand on his son. "What's going on? Why don't you want to come?"

Peter turns over and looks up at his father. "Well, I really am tired. But I suppose that's not all. Sometimes I get so bored. It seems like we hear the same lessons over and over again. I get tired of it, that's all."

Dad: "It can be pretty repetitive."

Son: "Yeah. I think I could teach those lessons myself."

Dad is quiet.

Son: "And sometimes I don't know what to think about what they have to say. Some of those stories are pretty hard for me to swallow."

Dad: "You're not sure if you believe everything you hear."

Son: "Yeah. That's kind of hard for me to admit, knowing how much faith you and Mom have and all. But sometimes I'm not so sure."

Dad: "I didn't know this."

Son: "I haven't told you. I've been afraid you'd be disappointed in me."

Dad: "No. I'm not disappointed. A little concerned but not disappointed. I recognize that you're thinking for yourself. You have to decide what you think. But I'd like to hear more."

Son: "Yeah."

Dad: "This is not the most convenient time because it is getting close to time to leave. But I'd like to talk later, if you're open."

Son: "I'd like that."

Dad: "Peter, can I tell you why it is important to me to go today?"

Son: "Sure."

Dad chokes up a little. "I go because I love to feel the Spirit. There's something, at least for me, about worship and participating in a holy ordinance that is touching. I cherish that time to do an inventory of my life and really communicate with my Father in Heaven. I usually come away feeling pretty uplifted."

Son: "I get that."

Dad stands up. "I'd love you to come with the family. But I think it's your decision." He looks at his watch. "We'll be leaving in half an hour. If you're up and out in the car, we'll go together. If not, we'll go without you." He turns and leaves the room.

## COMMENT

Although the fathers in all three of the teen scenarios love their sons, the father in the nurturing climate parents differently than the permissive or authoritarian father. Notice that he is engaged but not controlling. His intent is not simply to get his son up and ready for church. By his respect and care, he has opened up a deeper conversation. He asks questions and listens but also respects his son's will. He'll be honest about his own values and feelings but allow his son to have his opinions and be responsible for his own decisions.

This approach will ensure that father and son continue to have a strong relationship, with the father able to influence his son as he thinks about difficult questions and decisions. Such questions don't go away because we either avoid them (permissive approach) or force our answers (authoritarian approach). The art of being a nurturing parent is to be involved in a way that doesn't take responsibility away from our children.

## SUMMARY

Most of us grew up in homes that skewed either permissive or authoritarian. As I stated at the beginning of this chapter, not all were equally permissive or authoritarian. A family climate might vary from mild to extreme on either or both dimensions of demanding and responsive. Or, two parents may differ in their parenting styles, resulting in a mishmash of the two.

But take a moment—how would you characterize the home in which you grew up?

What about the climate in your family today? How does it resemble a permissive, authoritarian, or nurturing home? How would you like it to be?

My intent, as we continue, is to offer principles and skills to create a nurturing home. Not a perfect home, but one in which there is a proper balance of expectations and routine as well as emotional connection and respect.

# Family Climate Summary Chart

| Authoritarian Climate | Nurturing Climate |
|---|---|
| • Clear, authoritarian leadership of parents<br>• Lots of rules and punishment<br>• Routine and structure<br>• Lack of warmth or value for feelings<br>• Criticism—you cannot please others<br>• Parents over control through lecturing, prodding, reminding, etc.<br>• Only "good" feelings/opinions shared/accepted<br>• Children become defensive or quiet | • Proactive/authoritative leadership of parents<br>• Structure and routine that flow from principles<br>• Clear limits and enforcement with action and not lots of words or punishments<br>• Lots of communication; commitment to work things out<br>• Safe to share feelings/opinions<br>• Respect and trust for each family member<br>• Each person responsible for own actions |
| **Uninvolved Climate** | **Permissive Climate** |
| • Parents absent physically or mentally<br>• Few rules and expectations<br>• No consequences<br>• Lack of structure and routine<br>• Little emotional connection<br>• Lots of chaos—every person for self<br>• High independence and freedom | • Lack of parental authority<br>• Value independence<br>• Parents responsive to children's needs and feelings<br>• Few rules or not consistently enforced<br>• Disorganization and absence of structure<br>• Parents overindulge emotionally or materially<br>• Children often emotional and demanding<br>• Unclear or poorly enforced boundaries |

CHAPTER 3

# Nine Principles of a Nurturing Home

SOME PARENTS ARE INSTINCTIVELY ABLE to create a nurturing home. Many of us, however, will need to *deliberately* design our families to achieve that vision. The word "deliberate" means carefully thought out, done on purpose, premeditated, not rash or hasty (Webster's New World Dictionary).

This starts with understanding the principles of a nurturing climate. Principles are deeper than behavior and not directly observable. They can be thought of as fundamental and universal truths which we may draw upon to influence our behavior. We don't invent principles. We discover them and then seek to make our actions align to them. It works like this:

Principles ⟶ Behaviors ⟶ Outcomes

A nurturing home is an outcome that is predicated on certain behaviors. These behaviors are determined by principles. The more closely we can align our behavior to sound principles, the more closely we will approximate a nurturing home.

Therefore, there is power in being clear about the principles by which we'll govern our families. As we think deeply about principles and commit to live them, we become less reactive and better able to respond to the challenges of family life in ways that promote the development of our children.

I'm going to share nine principles of a nurturing home. I've identified them from research on successful families as well as observing what goes on in nurturing homes. I invite you to ponder them and decide if they make sense. Then consider specific behaviors (actions and communication) that align to these principles and which will be predictive of building a nurturing family climate.

## PRINCIPLE 1: WE, AS PARENTS, ARE THE AUTHORITY IN OUR HOMES.

Due to our knowledge, capability, and experience, we have a duty to preside in our homes. Children need guidance and boundaries. As parents, we have to have the strength to teach them good conduct and set and enforce appropriate limits. Loving parents are not mean, but they do say what they mean and mean what they say.

A problem in society today is that we've disempowered parents from being the authority in the home. My parents, part of the greatest generation, grew up in an authoritarian era. Children were to be seen and not heard. They had to mind or else. Following World War II the pendulum began a swing from authoritarianism to permissiveness due to the incredible growth of material prosperity and liberalization of social policies.

This isn't all bad. In fact, parents are more involved and have better relationships with their children today than ever before. But the pendulum has swung too far. Many parents are overly indulgent of their children, working too hard to keep them happy and make life easy. In the process, they oftentimes give up their authority.

Our goal is not to revert to an authoritarian model. Rather, it is to preside in our homes by establishing a positive family structure (routines, expectations, traditions), teaching our children appropriate behavior, and communicating in ways that instill personal responsibility.

## PRINCIPLE 2: OUR CHILDREN ARE INHERENTLY GOOD, CAPABLE, AND TRUSTWORTHY.

Our children come into the world underdeveloped physically, mentally, socially, and emotionally. Naturally they'll make poor choices and act in selfish and immature ways. We sometimes witness their poor choices or become exasperated by their immature behavior and conclude that they're bad, incapable, or untrustworthy. Unfortunately, this sets us up to interact with them as if this were the case. Instead of helping them learn and grow, we reinforce negative messages which all too easily become part of their identity.

We make it easier for our children to succeed if we believe in them; if we make positive rather than negative assumptions. Our most deeply held beliefs, conscious or unconscious, become self-fulfilling prophecies. Positive assumptions allow us to communicate and act from respect and trust, rather than fear and mistrust. Positive assumptions enable our children to build self-worth, grow in confidence, and make good choices.

Consider contrasting assumptions or beliefs:

* "My child is inherently good."
* "My child wants to do what is right."
* "My child is honest."
* "My child wants to get along with others."
* "My child is a capable student."
* "My child is imperfect and will make plenty of mistakes."
* "I can help my child learn and grow from her mistakes."

On the other hand:

* "Children will lie if they can get away with it."
* "Children are lazy and will do as little as possible."
* "Children don't care about others."
* "My kid is a pain."

We'll handle the same situation differently, depending on our core beliefs. Even when things go wrong, we'll be more successful as we make positive assumptions: Johnny is noisy, *not because he's bad*, but because he doesn't know how to channel his energy; Billy hits his brother because he is jealous; Suzie stayed out late past curfew because she has not yet figured out how to say "no" to friends. We are much more successful in addressing these issues when we see them through positive rather than negative lenses.

This principle is not about seeing with rose-colored glasses. It is not about denying real problems or expecting our children to be perfect. It is about seeing beneath the behavior to the heart, which may be covered over with layers of inadequacy and self-protection, and learning to trust and connect with the goodness deep within our children.

## PRINCIPLE 3: OUR CHILDREN LONG TO FEEL LOVE AND CONNECTION.

The need for love is universal and comes from our profound interdependence. Not only is a newborn totally dependent on his caregivers for survival, but even his sense of worth comes from the loving affection he receives from others. His physical needs may be met completely, but if a baby doesn't receive large doses of touch, cuddling, smiling, eye contact, and affirming words, he will likely grow up to be severely mentally or emotionally handicapped.

This longing for love continues throughout our lives, albeit in more disguised forms. So much of our striving for achievement and success is really about knowing that we matter, that we have worth to others. So many of our addictive and adrenalin seeking behaviors are escapes from our loneliness and lack of meaningful connection to others. Our relationships, more than any other factor, define our happiness and the quality of our lives. Connection and attachment give our lives its greatest meaning.

So we have a profound responsibility to help our children feel our love. There is no better way to inoculate them from the harsh transitions and storms of life than being emotionally safe, sensitive, and responsive to their needs and inner experience. There is no better way to help them feel good about themselves than offering our non-possessive care and attention.

Of course, this is not easy to do. Love, by its very nature, cannot be forced. We can offer the gift of our love but our children must open their hearts to receive it. Even loving parents have children who make poor choices and stray from family values, for many reasons.

Likewise, we, as parents, are only human. We have demands and stresses in our lives that make it impossible to always be present in loving ways for our children (even for ourselves). Furthermore, we grew up with imperfect role models and so wrestle with own our issues of adequacy and intimacy. Here we are, adults, still trying to satisfy our own hunger for love and meaning while providing the best we can for our children.

But knowing that our children long for love can help us immensely. Perhaps we can reframe much of their bad behavior as a flawed attempt to seek connection. Perhaps we can commit to finding more ways of offering connection—our time, affection, playfulness, deep listening, praise, respect, and non-judgment. After all, we draw our children to us and influence them far more through positive interactions than by punishing, criticizing, and nagging.

## PRINCIPLE 4: WE ARE RESPONSIBLE "TO" BUT NOT "FOR" OUR CHILDREN.

This is a critical distinction. As parents, we certainly have many responsibilities "to" our children. We are responsible to provide them shelter, food, safety, instruction, correction, love, and so on. But we cross a boundary when we make ourselves responsible "for" them. We have now set ourselves up to fix, solve, protect, rescue, and control their behavior and emotions. This is a losing battle that not only violates the principle of personal responsibility but causes us untold worry, strife, and anguish.

Notice the difference in how we parent when we are clear about our responsibility "to" rather than "for":

| If I feel *responsible for* my children, I... | If I feel *responsible to* my children, I... |
|---|---|
| • Fix, solve, protect, rescue, and control | • Listen, encourage, support, love |
| • Feel tired, worried, fearful, unappreciated | • Feel relaxed, trusting, confident, appreciated |
| • Expect them to live up to my expectations | • Trust them to live up to their own expectations |
| • Manipulate them to make sure things turn out right | • Am concerned with enjoying our relationship |

(Adapted from R. Lerner and B. Naditch, *Children Are People*, workshop manual)

By being responsible "for," we rob our children of their own responsibility and steal from them growth opportunities of great value. By being responsible "to," we help them become independent and carry out their own age-appropriate responsibilities, solve their own problems, and make their own choices. However, learning to do this takes great trust and faith. It requires that we focus less on our children and more on our own assumptions and emotional reactions.

## PRINCIPLE 5: OUR CHILDREN ARE RESPONSIBLE FOR THEMSELVES.

Individual responsibility is a fundamental principle of life. Our children are not "ours" but belong to themselves and, ultimately, must be accountable for themselves. We can teach and guide. We can't, however, click a remote and compel them to think and do exactly as we want. They "own" their lives and have to make their own choices.

And yet, I speak from experience when I say that it is easy to violate the principle of individual responsibility by over controlling our children. Because we want our children to make good choices, we lecture, nag, remind, criticize, threaten, shame, and manipulate. Or, we overprotect and rescue them from their choices or do for them what they should be able to do for themselves. These tactics are truly well-intentioned. We use them because we care. But they impose control from without rather than building responsibility from within. And they often breed dependency, ill will, or resentment and prevent our children from developing conviction and the ability to govern themselves.

We help our children learn responsibility in many ways. We do so as we create nurturing homes. We do so as we set an example of making and keeping commitments and promises. We do so when we set limits and enforce their consequences. We do so as we let them make age-appropriate decisions. We do so as we allow them to experience the consequences of their decisions or behavior without rescuing them. We do so as we expect them to do for themselves instead of doing for them. We do so as we create safe and trusting conditions and let them open up and tell us what is on their minds. We do so as we learn to ask questions rather than solve problems for them. Ultimately, teaching and allowing our children to assume responsibility for themselves is at the heart of effective parenting.

## PRINCIPLE 6: GROWTH REQUIRES EFFORT AND EVEN STRUGGLE.

Life is not easy. It not only places demands on us but also includes some degree of mental, physical, or emotional suffering. This fact is a truth, simply what is.

Our children begin to experience the difficulties of life at an early age. They get tired. Things don't go their way. Mom is cranky and reactive (sometimes even mean). Other kids are bigger, have nicer toys, or are better in school. Learning takes effort. Being social includes rejection.

And yet this is the pathway of growth. By facing adversity and the challenges of daily life, we gain faith, courage, discipline, and character. It is the means by which we discover our strength, develop emotional resilience, and achieve our potential.

Nevertheless, it can be painful to watch our kids struggle. Or we don't fully trust their capability or know healthy ways of supporting them and so we intervene to make life easier for them. We help the toddler onto the couch instead of letting him struggle to climb up on his own. We overreact when a child falls and scrapes a knee. We fail to give children chores. We do too much of their homework. We call the school to adjust a schedule. By so doing, we weaken them and foster an entitlement mentality. We fail to help them deal with the realities and daily responsibilities of their lives.

I've heard a consistent message from leaders of youth, such as employers, teachers, student advisors, and administrators of universities. Many youth have led an easy life. They lack a good work ethic and don't know how to do hard things. Many young people lack discipline.

I believe two factors account for this. First is an affluent lifestyle. So much is available to make life easy and convenient that didn't exist in past generations. Second is the incredible rise of technology that puts not only information but entertainment at our fingertips. These are blessings and maladies. Many youth don't have to work for what they get and there is a never-ending stream of distractions and entertainment available to them. So they don't learn to wait. They don't experience as much delay of gratification as past generations. They don't value the connection between their own hard-earned efforts and rewards.

Life does not offer us a free ride. Likewise, we shouldn't feel guilty about letting our children struggle to learn the lessons of life (as though they could live forever in a state of unending bliss). Children need to learn the discipline of doing hard things. They need to learn to tolerate frustration, deal with disappointment, and delay gratification, qualities that predict success.

As parents, we know that life won't be easy for our kids. Yet we need to trust them and give them the space to struggle and figure life out. We can support them in this process (as I'll teach in upcoming chapters), but not if we feel sorry and want to make it too easy for them.

## PRINCIPLE 7: LIMITS AND CONSEQUENCES
### TEACH WISDOM AND RESPONSIBILITY.

Parents exercise authority by setting limits and allowing children to learn from consequences. Don't come to dinner when called and go hungry. Forget an assignment and get marked down. Don't hold a job, can't buy a car. What doesn't work is getting mad or feeling overly responsible when our children don't do what we'd like. What does work is allowing them to experience the consequences of their choices. Our children learn wisdom and responsibility through limits and consequences (not preaching and nagging).

This is particularly important when children are young. I believe in the V principle of parenting. This means that we provide more structure in the form of clear boundaries and consequences when children are young and then allow our children to be more and more self-governing as they get older. Some parents invert the V: ∧. They are lax when their children are young and then have to impose more control as they get older. This often sets children up to rebel or continually test limits. On the other hand, if they learn about limits and consequences at a young age, they become more self-regulating and don't need so many rules and limits as they get older.

It is not my place to tell parents where to set boundaries. These will differ between families. Some families are more strict and some more liberal. Perhaps even more important than the boundaries is their enforcement. Wherever we set our boundaries, it is important that we enforce them with actions (not words). Most of us give away our power by lecturing, pleading, and reminding instead of taking action. Children need to know that we will act when they violate a boundary, act immediately, consistently, without anger, and without guilt or pity.

What we're really doing is teaching our children the way the world works. We make choices and there are consequences (some long term and some short term). As adults, we learn to make good choices because of the consequences. We teach our children the same principle as we establish and follow through with consequences on little, day-to-day things.

## PRINCIPLE 8: SUCCESSFUL PARENTING REQUIRES THAT WE GROW OURSELVES FIRST.

The biggest challenge to parenting is not our children's behavior but our own emotional reactivity. When reactive, we regress to immature words and actions, causing our children to be defensive and self-protective, so they fail to learn from their mistakes. Loving parenting is not about getting our children to be different. It starts with getting ourselves to be different. Children need parents who are calm and loving and yet firm and consistent.

Unfortunately, we rely more on lecturing, nagging, scolding, and criticizing than positive communication skills to teach and motivate our children. We use these strategies because we get an immediate reward. The noxious behavior of our children stops…but only temporarily. Negative, reactive communication begets negative, reactive attitudes and behavior from our children. We've set up a vicious cycle in which we reinforce the very behaviors we want to eliminate.

So we need to learn to pause and focus more on our own responses (which we do control) rather than the behavior of our children (which we can influence but not control). We do this in three ways. We learn to ignore many annoying, attention-seeking behaviors—bickering, sulking, fussing, and complaining. We focus on changing what we can control (enforcing consequences) rather than behaviors and moods of our children. And we utilize positive, strengthening communication strategies that help our children mature and take greater responsibility for their behavior.

By changing ourselves, our relationships change. If we are less volatile, our children relax. If we are less defensive, we make it easier for our children to talk to us. If we respect ourselves, we set boundaries and teach our children to treat us with respect. By changing how we communicate, our family members will respond in a different way. If we're coming from a healthier place, our family dynamics are inevitably going to improve.

This means that we need to look at our part in the dynamics of the relationship. What are we doing that is working and not working? We let go of our defensiveness so we can see how we may be contributing to the behavior we don't like in our children. This isn't self-blame. It's meekness. It's a willingness to be taught by others, even our children.

The important question about parenting is not whether we're parenting in the right way but rather if we are being the adult we want our children to become. Who we are, not just as parents but as people, will have a more lasting influence on our children than our theories and techniques. So parenting is a journey in which growing ourselves is our highest priority.


## PRINCIPLE 9: WE ARE IMPERFECT (AND THAT IS OKAY).

We are imperfect. Likewise, our children are imperfect. This is a fact, part of the nature of life.

We do harm to ourselves and our children when we believe that we have to be perfect in order to be lovable. This causes us to put unrealistic expectations on ourselves—to always know what to do or to behave maturely in every moment. We still fall short. So we work even harder to be (or at least appear) perfect through various forms of performing, pleasing, proving, or pretending, which, paradoxically, only separates us more from the feelings of love and acceptance we desire.

Of course, our perfectionism spills over to our children. They get the message that they have to be a certain way—smart enough, pretty enough, cool enough, athletic enough, quiet enough—to have our love. They conclude that they aren't loved for who they are but for who we want them to be. Some learn to conform and/or perform in ways that please us. Others conclude they'll never please us. Some rebel. Others retreat. All live with a sense of not being enough.

Parenting isn't about perfection. It is about having the courage to be vulnerable and soft-hearted so we can take responsibility and grow from our mistakes. Growing is not about covering up our weaknesses but being real and admitting them. As we bring our flaws to the light of day, let ourselves be seen as imperfect, honor our vulnerability, and talk about our struggles (as well as our strengths), we become more loving and mature.

As we accept ourselves as imperfect, we become more accepting and forgiving of our children. We let them be imperfect. Then we can be a safe place for them to talk, explore, "own" and work through their mistakes. As we practice compassion with ourselves, we allow our children to practice it with themselves and each other. They learn they can open their hearts and talk about the hard things. They learn that they are enough.

## SUMMARY

I began this chapter by talking about the importance of principles. Understanding correct principles leads to good behavior, which leads to good outcomes. It looks like this:

| Principles ⟶ | Behavior ⟶ | Outcomes |
|---|---|---|
| | | A nurturing climate in which our children: |
| 1. We are the authority in our homes. | | |
| 2. Our children are inherently good, capable, and trustworthy. | | • Know of their goodness and worth |
| 3. Our children long to feel love and connection. | | • Feel safe enough to talk |
| 4. We are responsible "to" but not "for" our children. | (stay tuned) | • Delay gratification and tolerate frustration |
| | | • Act rather than react |
| 5. Our children are responsible for themselves. | | • Solve problems and make good decisions |
| 6. Growth requires effort, even struggle. | | • Set and work toward goals |
| 7. Limits and consequences teach wisdom and responsibility. | | • Make and keep commitments |
| | | • Act from a moral and spiritual compass |
| 8. Successful parenting requires that we grow ourselves first. | | • Respect and cooperate with others |
| 9. We're imperfect (and that's okay). | | |

By understanding correct principles we become more confident about how to act and communicate in a given situation. As we act in positive ways, aligned with true principles, we produce better outcomes, create a nurturing family climate, and raise responsible, emotionally mature children.

So, I'd like to invite you to take some time to ponder these principles. In fact, write them down (or make a copy) and carry them with you. Do you agree with them? What do they mean to you, personally? How would you modify them to make them your own? Which do you live today? Which could you improve in?

Then do an "if...then" exercise. "If I fully understand and internalize x principle (fill in the blank), then how will I behave? What will I think and do, consistently, to practice and demonstrate my belief in this principle?"

The next chapters are about behavior. What behaviors are negative and weakening, not aligned with true principles, and lead us away from a nurturing home? What behaviors are positive and strengthening and help us create a nurturing home and responsible children?

Let's find out.

# CHAPTER 4

# Weakening Versus
# Strengthening Interactions

A LOT OF PARENTING GOES on day-to-day as we casually interact with our kids. Most of these interactions have to do with managing life and proceed without incident. Some interactions, however, are more significant because of the potential learning inherent within them.

I call these interactions **key moments**. A key moment is a situation or event that presents a challenge and requires a response. In fact, we cannot *not* respond to a key moment. The question is, are we conscious and aware as we respond, or do we simply react in a knee-jerk kind of way? Do we respond in ways that are weakening or strengthening?

Here are examples of key moments.

- Fifth grader announces: "I hate school and I'm never going back"
- Son refuses to get off the couch and help with chores
- Daughter brings home a really bad report card
- Teenager is out past curfew
- Child dilly-dallies rather than getting ready for school
- Kids bicker and argue every evening at the dinner table
- Son throws a fit when you tell him his screen time is over
- Daughter is pouty and refuses to spend time with family
- Son comes home late and has been drinking

Such key moments are important because our children learn lessons depending upon how we respond. When we handle such key moments poorly, we interfere with our children's ability to learn from their experiences and make good decisions. Handling them well means we're behaving and communicating in ways that promote their growth and development.

We have key moments every day. Some are minor and we handle them easily. Others, however, are (or seem) big and trigger negative emotions (fear, anger, exacerbation, powerlessness) that knock us off balance, make us forget our vision or principles, diminish our enjoyment of our kids, and cause us to react in unproductive and weakening ways. Here is what happens:

## The Key Moment Model

An event occurs and, consciously or unconsciously, we make a choice about how to respond. If unaware or if strong emotions overrule our reason, we're likely to react from fear or hostility, leading us into a "Cycle of Weakening Behavior" in which we either over manage or overindulge our children. As the diagram illustrates, negative (usually unintended) consequences flow from these behaviors—ill will, mistrust and power struggles, low self-esteem, diminishing of personal responsibility, problems go unsolved, etc.

Unfortunately, it is all too easy to get cycled into these weakening behaviors, which rob children of their ability to be self-governing and cause them to be externally driven. As the diagram to the right illustrates, these reactions impose control on our children from without rather than building responsibility and self-discipline from within.

On the other hand, we can choose to respond to a key moment from faith, love, and trust (not always easy). As we do so, we interact with our children in ways that are strengthening to them as well as our relationship. The goal is more than getting compliance or solving the immediate problem. It's to build trust, enhance self-worth, help children think for themselves, solve problems, and take responsibility for their thoughts, feelings, and actions (inside out rather than outside in). The consequences are goodwill, trust, enhanced self-worth, and an increase in personal responsibility and ability of a child to manage his life.

Notice that there are three skill sets at the top of the Key Moment Model: Honesty, Empathy, and Responsibility. From many years of experience, I've learned that these core skills are the heart of good communication at any time, and particularly in the middle of a key moment. I'll define them and teach you how to use them in the upcoming chapters. In the meantime, I want to continue exploring what happens during the "Cycle of Weakening Behavior."

From the Key Moment Model, you can see that there are two types of weakening behaviors. First is **over managing**. We do this in many ways:

**Lecturing:** Moralizing and telling children how to think, feel, and act, which builds resentment and deprives them of the opportunity to think for themselves.

**Arguing:** Getting caught up in verbal battles, trying to convince each other that we're "right" and they are "wrong," which only leads to more entrenched positions.

**Criticizing:** Finding fault and making negative comments about their character or behavior to try to get them to do what we want.

**Getting Mad:** Yelling, hitting, fuming, etc. Expresses parent's powerlessness and causes the child to feel resentment and shame.

**Giving Advice ("nifty plans"):** Telling kids what to do or how to solve their problems. It will usually be rejected. Even if accepted, it breeds dependency and lack of faith in self.

**Comparing:** Pointing out differences between one child and another to either make him feel good or get him to change.

**Blaming:** Accusing another of negative motives or attributing a negative situation to her.

**Threatening:** Verbally expressing an intention to impose a severe consequence on a child, often with no intent to carry it out.

**Nagging:** Constantly scolding, reminding, or complaining to get a child to do what you want.

All of these tactics are ways of taking over and manipulating our children to do what we want. We use them when we feel fearful and anxious and lose our trust in the natural goodness and capability of children. The tactics either cause our children to become compliant (good boy/girl) or rebel (bad boy/girl). Either way, over managing keeps our children from taking responsibility for themselves. Plus, it plants subtle and harmful messages in the minds of our children, such as:

* "You think I'm bad or stupid or inferior."
* "You don't care about my feelings or will. You just want me to please you."
* "You don't trust me to work this out on my own."

The second form of weakening response to a key moment is **overindulging,** which also has many forms.

**Hovering:** Being overly aware and responsive to a child's every move. Failure to allow her the physical or emotional space to make choices or act on her own.

**Sympathizing:** Communicating pity for what a child is going through. Different from empathy. Rewards him for feeling bad rather than taking action.

**Avoiding:** Withdrawing into ourselves and leaving our children without support, structure, or guidance because we are uncertain or overwhelmed by their needs.

**Catering:** Giving in to a child's whims and wishes. Bending over backward to keep him happy or making sure that things go his way so he won't be upset.

**Fixing:** Solving a problem or doing for a child what she could and should be able to do for herself—making a bed, choosing clothes, talking to a teacher.

**Rescuing:** Trying to make a child feel better by undoing consequences or not allowing a child to face the consequences of his actions or choices.

**Protecting:** Preventing a child from facing the realities of life by not letting her engage in experiences that involve social, emotional, or even physical risk.

**Flip-flopping:** Setting a boundary and then renegotiating because it was not convenient, the kids pushed back, or you thought you were being harsh.

**Pleading:** Begging kids to do what you want rather than expecting and letting them be responsible.

**Bribing:** Making a promise to do something or give the child something to get him to do what you want, something he should probably be doing anyway.

**Giving in:** Wearing down as you hear whining or complaints. Letting a child do/have what she wants to avoid enforcing a boundary. It is easier.

When we overindulge, we give children too much power or reward their bad behavior rather than letting them face consequences and learn responsibility. We are trying to keep them happy and so end up giving away our parental authority. Children get messages like:

* "I have to get my way to feel okay."
* "Limits don't apply to me."
* "Someone else will make things all better."
* "No one is more powerful than me."

If you have ever watched an episode of *Super Nanny,* then you've seen other examples of parents who overindulge. They don't know how to set limits and be firm. They want to please their children and ensure that they're always happy and so end up giving away their authority. The Nanny's goal is to help the parents in these families accept their authority, learn to set limits, work together as a couple, and take charge of what is going on at home.

## WEAKENING BEHAVIOR—AN EXAMPLE

Here's an example of a key moment. Let's watch two parents respond to their son in weakening, although different, ways.

John Carlson was doing well in school until Mrs. Bowman's eighth-grade English class. John failed the class and came home despondent, afraid to tell his mother what had happened. Mrs. Carlson probed John about what was going on and finally heard his forced, halted confession. She then said: "That teacher should not have done that to you. She is so unfair. Her expectations are simply not realistic. Besides, you're a good student. Don't you worry, I'm going to talk to Mrs. Bowman and see what I can do."

How common is this reaction? Is Mother's sympathy helping or hurting? What is John learning? What kinds of habits are forming between John and his mother?

John's father came home a few hours later. When his wife told him about John's grade, Mr. Carlson rushed into John's room, making the following declarations: "How can you bring home an F in English? Your brothers never got Fs in any subject. I've been telling you your priorities are messed up, and I've had enough of it, young man. No more Xbox or TV until further notice. And, by the way, you're grounded from your friends until I know that your grade has improved."

Now what is happening? What are the consequences? Is it more likely to be helpful or harmful to John?

There is no doubt that John's parents have good intent. They love their son and want him to succeed. In fact, it's usually because we care deeply that we step into parenting traps that are weakening. We're doing our best to get our kids to do what we believe they should be doing. However, we don't see how we're robbing them of self-responsibility in the process.

## MORE EXAMPLES

Here are a few more key moments. As you read them, think about the parental responses and why they are weakening rather than strengthening.

| Situation | Over managing | Overindulging |
|---|---|---|
| Fifth grader announces: "I hate school and I'm never going back." | • "You don't hate school. You just had a bad day." <br> • "Oh yes you are, mister. Don't you talk like that around here." <br> • "What trouble did you get into now?" | • "Come here. Some cookies and milk will help you feel better." <br> • "Oh, I feel so bad to hear you talk that way." |
| Son refuses to get off the couch and help with chores. | • "How many times do I have to tell you to help? I'm sick of asking." <br> • "Get off the couch and start doing your part, and I mean NOW!" <br> • "You are grounded until further notice." | • "Please, Jess. I try so hard to keep you guys happy and it seems like it's never enough." <br> • "Listen, I'll do your chores tonight, but you have to promise that you'll work extra on Saturday." |
| Daughter is pouty and refuses to spend time with family. | • "You change your attitude right now or you won't go out this weekend." <br> • Father grabs daughter. "Get over here and start acting like you're human." | • "You don't know how it hurts me when you won't spend time with us. I feel like a terrible mother." <br> • "Are you feeling bad again? I'm so sorry you're unhappy." |

# WHY WE DO WHAT WE DO

Although aware that the consequences of over managing and overindulging our children are harmful, we slip into these patterns for a number of reasons.

First, we're unaware of what's happening. We've not had a framework or language to understand what's going on in our interactions. We don't see the relationship between our behavior and its consequences.

Second, we get hooked emotionally when our kids are behaving in self-ish, immature, or threatening ways. The feelings happen so quickly that we're hardly aware of them before we're acting out of fear or anger. It seems almost impossible to override the emotion with a more rational response.

Third, we get payoffs out of these behaviors. By payoffs, I'm talking about short-term rewards that reinforce our weakening responses. A mother who yells gets compliance. A father who gives in doesn't have to deal with whining (at least for the moment). We get short-term rewards for reacting the way we do.

A final reason we use these strategies is that we don't know a better way. We're likely to be doing something similar to the way we were raised. It seems natural. We haven't learned that there may be a set of skills which we can learn that will lead to better outcomes.

# MAKING A NEW CHOICE

Remember the popular definition of insanity? (Continuing to do what we've been doing and expecting a different result.) If we want different results, then we have to behave in a different way. The Key Moment Model suggests that there is a moment of choice when we make a decision about how to respond to a key moment. If unconscious we don't have a choice. We simply react. But as we become more aware, we begin to realize that our responses don't have to be automatic. We can choose to respond in ways that help our children learn and grow in responsibility and emotional maturity.

In the next chapter, we'll take a deeper look at our key moments and learn principles and a technique for handling them so we're in a better place emotionally to use the skills of honesty, empathy, and responsibility.

# CHAPTER 5

# Parenting with a Soft Heart

IN CHAPTER 3, I STATED that the biggest challenge to our parenting is not our children's behavior but our own emotional reactivity. Many of our natural reactions (controlling, yelling, criticizing, rescuing, bribing, giving in) prevent us from responding to our children in positive ways. Unfortunately, when we get "hooked" and react, we set up a vicious cycle in which our children become all the more defensive, self-justifying, and/or protective. They fail to learn from their experiences and we end up feeling as though we're failing as parents.

Parenting with a soft heart is not soft parenting. It means that we start with ourselves, our own hearts, so we can respond to our children in ways that enable them to grow in responsibility and emotional maturity. When we do so, the skills of honesty, empathy, and responsibility, which we'll learn in upcoming chapters, come quite easily. If our hearts are not soft, we fail to use the skills, not because we don't understand them, but because our emotions override our reasoning.

When "hard-hearted" we act from pride. We're defensive and self-justifying. We are focused on how a child is the problem and needs to change. We fail to see our part in what's happening or, better yet, how we can alter our own perceptions and communication in ways that help our children learn and grow.

It takes a soft and humble heart to recognize that what *we* are doing may not be working and that we need to change our approach (rather than simply trying to get our children to be different.) Whenever we're stuck, whenever we don't like what is going on in our relationships with our children, the place to start is with ourselves. After all, our children don't make us react the way we do. We make choices.

The purpose of this chapter is to take a deeper look at those key moments when we get "hooked" and react in unhealthy ways. By becoming aware, taking responsibility for our emotional reactions, and learning to make new choices during our key moments, we grow emotionally and also create an environment in which our children can learn and thrive.

## KEY MOMENTS

We discussed the Key Moment Model in the last chapter. A key moment is an upsetting situation or event. Consciously or unconsciously, we make choices during our key moments, and our effectiveness depends upon our ability to make strengthening rather than weakening choices. When we respond negatively, we slip into the "Cycle of Weakening Behavior" by over managing and/ or overindulging our children. These responses harm trust and our ability to influence our children. When we respond positively, we move into the "Cycle of Strengthening Behavior" by using the skills of honesty, empathy, and responsibility. We thereby build trust and help our children learn and become more mature.

The following diagram offers more detail about what happens during a key moment.

**Triggering event:** Most key moments are triggered by an event or situation (child sasses, comes home late, or refuses to do homework).

**Thoughts:** The "spin" we put on our key moments; the conclusions we arrive at to make sense of what is happening. These thoughts are usually spontaneous, unconscious, negative, and yet believable. They may be linked with memories from the past or visual images about the "worst possible outcome."

**Feelings:** What we experience inside our bodies. There are two types of feelings that accompany a key moment:

> **Physical sensations:** Shortness of breath, muscle tension, dry mouth, nausea, etc.
>
> **Emotions:** Anger, hurt, sadness, helplessness, fear, inadequacy, etc.

**Behavior:** What we do. Our behavior can be positive and strengthening or negative and weakening. Our natural tendency is to dramatize or act out our grungy, negative feelings by either over controlling or overindulging.

**Consequences:** The outcomes or effect of our behavior on us and our children. When we respond poorly to key moments, the consequences become lose/lose propositions and set the stage for more triggering events.

Understanding the elements of a key moment helps us make better choices. After all, we can't change if we're on automatic pilot. It's necessary that we "wake up" and pay attention to our triggering events and our subsequent thoughts, feelings, behavior, and consequences. Taking responsibility for these choices and learning to make better choices is the price we pay to improve our relationships and better influence our children.

So think about a recent, or recurring, key moment. What do your children do/ not do or say that triggers you? Then answer the questions on the next page to become aware of how you typically respond. Such awareness is the gateway to making better choices. (A copy of this exercise is found in Appendix F, page 151, so you can print extra copies.)

# Key Moment Exercise

1. **Event**
   a.  What happened?

   b.  What, specifically, about the event triggered your reaction?

2. **Thoughts**
   c.  How did you interpret the event?

   d.  What negative thoughts about your children or the event caused you to react?

3. **Feelings**
   e.  What physical sensations did you experience?

   f.  What emotions did you feel?

4. **Behavior**
   g.  What did you do during the key moment?

   h.  What did you do afterwards?

5. **Consequences**
   i.  What were the immediate consequences of how you reacted?

    j.   What are the long-term consequences?

6.  As you look back, how are you feeling about how you handled this key moment?

7.  What might you do differently in the future?

# THE MOMENT OF CHOICE

The moment of choice is a moment of awareness and personal power when we make a conscious decision to interrupt our negative reactions and make new and strengthening choices during our key moments.

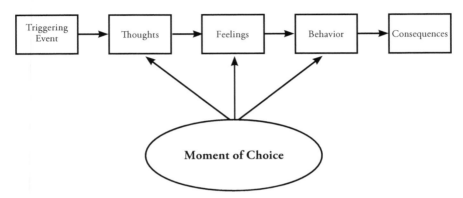

We can interrupt any of the elements of a key moment. We might challenge our thoughts, alter our emotions (by going for a walk, listening to music, talking to a friend), or deliberately change our behavior by using one of the parenting skills. Making a change anywhere along the response chain shifts our entire experience.

Recognizing our key moments and the moment of choice is a process. At first, we find that many key moments happen so quickly that we aren't even aware of what's going on until later. In such instances, it's helpful to "circle back" and process a key moment after it's over. Much of our learning will take place after the fact.

As we become more aware, we begin to recognize when we're in the middle of a key moment, although we may feel that we have no control over our gut reactions. We may still need to process what happened following the event. Over time, we begin to anticipate our key moments and program ourselves to respond in more strengthening ways *before* they occur. And eventually, we don't need to think through all the steps in a mechanical way. We'll spontaneously make positive choices during challenging situations.

So be patient. Allow this to be a process in which you improve over time. You're reprogramming yourself to respond in new ways, which will take practice. Give yourself permission to "blow it" at times. Your purpose is to make progress, not achieve perfection.

The most important thing, in order to respond in better ways, is to keep the focus on ourselves and not our children. Initially, our goal should be to alter how we handle a key moment rather than trying to change our children. As we become less reactive, as we learn to make strengthening choices, we are making it possible for our children to learn and respond in more positive ways as well.

## THE MOMENT OF CHOICE—AN EXAMPLE

A story from a friend of mine illustrates the power of the moment of choice. One evening Jack went into his son's bedroom to have a talk. Before long, the conversation grew more contentious, and he and his son began arguing. It continued to escalate until the son said, "Dad, what I'd really like right now is to talk to my pastor."

Jack's immediate thought was, *Finally! That's the best idea this boy has had all evening.* Another realization quickly followed. *I am his pastor.*

Soberly, Jack excused himself and walked into the hallway. He stood for a moment, regaining his composure. He said a silent prayer and mentally took upon him the mantle of pastor. He returned to his son's room, sat on his bed and apologized for the way he had handled himself. He then said, "You're now talking to your pastor. Let's continue this conversation."

His son continued talking but now, instead of arguing, Jack listened. It was difficult. He didn't like much of what he was hearing and had to bite his tongue to avoid reacting. He responded as he would to a member of his congregation. By the end of the conversation, Jack and his son stood and embraced. They had achieved a depth of communication and closeness that they had not experienced in years.

This story is instructive. How often the words or behavior of our children trigger pretty deep emotions of fear, insecurity, powerlessness, or anger. It is so easy to do or say something weakening rather than strengthening. Yet Jack was able, within a few minutes, to alter his "psychology" (thoughts, feelings, and behavior) and completely change his approach. At a moment of choice, he shook off his natural responses and put himself in a more empowering frame of mind, adopting a new perspective, wisdom, behaviors, and feelings.

We can do the same. Although not easy, with desire and practice we can become aware of what is happening and learn to change our personal "psychology" and make better choices when in the middle of a key moment.

## STOP–LOOK–LISTEN–CHOOSE

There are many tools we can use to respond rather than react to our key moments. We can take deep breaths, count to ten, alter our posture or physical stance, take a momentary time out, recall our principles, pray, challenge our negative thinking, and so on. The goal is to draw upon resources or techniques that can help us assume a more positive state of mind.

Stop—Look—Listen—Choose is one such tool that I'd like to introduce. It's a structured process which we can use to stop our negative energy and choose more helpful responses.

**Stop** is the first step and has to do with recognizing that something harmful is happening. It requires a decision to refuse to act out in a harmful way. It sometimes helps to do something to change our physiology, such as breathing deeply, relaxing our face or torso, stretching, or softening our eyes. Jack altered his physiology by leaving his son's room and walking into the hallway. He took a moment to compose himself and alter his emotional state.

**Look** is the second step. This is noticing our thoughts, feelings, and behavior but without acting them out. Initially, I recommend using the Key Moment Exercise from earlier in the chapter to write down and explore our key moments. Although it seems cumbersome, writing slows the process, expands our awareness, and empowers us to take responsibility for our reactions.

Of course, we can't do this in the middle of a key moment. However, our most troubling key moments are recurring, so we can write between events. Writing takes discipline and even courage. But by taking time to go through this process, our negative feelings give way to stillness, insight, and personal power. It is how we choose to act rather than react.

I recommend spending a little more time with question two (thoughts) from the Key Moment Exercise. Inevitably, our thinking during our key moments is driven by automatic, negative thoughts. We can challenge these thoughts by learning to see their distortions:

- **Oversimplifying**—seeing our child in black-and-white terms
- **Mind-reading**—assuming we know what's going on without checking it out
- **Filtering**—dwelling on a single detail, usually negative, until it influences our entire vision (like putting a drop of ink in a beaker of water)
- **Catastrophizing**—making events worse than they really are
- **Fortune-telling**—predicting the future, which we really can't know
- **Personalizing**—believing it's our fault when things go wrong

Most negative thoughts have two or three distortions. By being alert to them, we become more positive and learn to think in a clear and calm way.

**Listen** is step three. We listen to our heart, our deeper wisdom. We think about our higher vision. What is most important in the long run? What outcomes do we want from this situation? Clarifying outcomes is extremely powerful. It is so much easier to react when we lack clarity. That is when we allow negative feelings and motives (defensiveness, over control, emotional reactivity, manipulation, getting even) to take over. On the other hand, being clear about the outcomes we desire (for ourselves, our child, and our relationships) empowers our higher, spiritual self and gives us the wisdom to know how to respond.

**Choose** is the final step. This step is moving into action. It begins by identifying choices that coincide with our vision or desired outcomes. These choices not only have to do with actions but our thoughts and feelings as well. How can we look at the situation differently? How can we change how we feel? And what actions can we take that will lead to positive results? Many of these new actions will be to use the communication skills I'll be teaching in the next few chapters.

Stop–Look–Listen–Choose provides a structure that enables us to be much more deliberate in handling our key moments. Some key moments can be resolved rather quickly by following this process. Others are deeply ingrained habits that developed over years and will require time to overcome. Practice makes perfect. Initially, we need to think through the steps and even write them down. As we remain conscious and keep at it, we will learn to respond in better and better ways.

## A Personal Example

It was late May and my family and I were seated around the dinner table talking about the upcoming summer. The kids were excited that they would soon be out of school, and, as a conscientious father, I was determined that Judy and I would help them use their time wisely. Certainly, in my mind, they should have plenty of time to play and have fun, but I didn't want the summer to be a free ride. I wanted to set up a routine that would require them to do chores and be involved in worthwhile activities.

I shared my ideas by saying that I thought they should be out of bed by 8:00 every morning and couldn't play until they had done their chores for the day. My twelve-year-old daughter, Melinda, responded with vehemence: "No, that's not fair. We have been going to school every day and getting up early, doing homework at night, and I need a break. I don't think I should have to be up by 8:00. I want to sleep in. And why do I have to do my work before I can play? Why can't I do my work when I want to do it?"

I was taken aback. Here was my oldest child, not even a teenager yet, openly defying me. I argued, "Melinda, how can you react this way? I'm not asking that much. You can sleep in until 8:00 and longer on Saturdays, which is a lot later than during the school year. You don't have that many chores. Most of the day you can do what you want. Besides, I don't get a vacation. I still have to get up early and go to work every day. Think about me." (Poor dad.)

She continued to argue and I wouldn't have it. I startled my kids as I brought my fist down on the table, ended the conversation, sent everyone to their rooms, and stormed off to the bedroom to stew about what had just happened.

At first, I built my case, how I was right and she was wrong. How I was the parent and she was the child. How my expectations were reasonable and for her good. In the process, not only did I lose my feelings of love towards Melinda, but I failed to deal with a more real issue—my underlying insecurities that caused me to react in anger. So, with the support of my wife, I did a version of Stop–Look–Listen–Choose (although I was not using these words back then).

Stop: I stopped the flow of negative feelings by lying on the bed and taking some deep breaths. I soon began to feel more relaxed and calm.

Look: I looked at my negative feelings and thoughts, not just the surface but deeper—my resentment about not being in control; my fear of Melinda growing up and making her own decisions; my embarrassment and sense of inadequacy for losing my cool. My wife listened as I explored my thoughts and their distortions. "That was a disaster" (catastrophizing) became "I didn't handle that well." "Melinda is being defiant" (mind-reading and oversimplifying) gave way to "She's growing older and wants more control over her life." "I'm not able to influence my kids" (oversimplifying) became "My kids and I have a good relationship. They want to learn from me." "If Melinda is so defiant at twelve, how will she be at sixteen?" (fortune-telling) became "It is good and right for my kids to think for themselves. I want to stay close to them and help them explore what they believe and what is important to them."

In short, I had to explore my deeper feelings and fears about my kids growing up and becoming more independent. This was a core fear. If unexamined, I would have continued to act this fear out whenever my kids made decisions I didn't like.

Listen: I asked myself questions. What is important to me? What do I really want? What is my vision of my relationship with the kids? I recognized that I wanted a good relationship with the kids. I wanted them to trust me and feel like they could talk to me. I recognized that the dynamics of our family were changing. The kids were growing up and starting to think for themselves more. They would be more assertive. I wanted to trust them and have an open relationship so we could talk.

Choose: I needed to make things right. A few days later we assembled again and I brought up the topic of our last discussion. I confessed that I'd not handled it well and that I wanted to talk things through, as we had differences of opinion, rather than shut down the conversation. I then spoke to Melinda: "You didn't react well to the schedule I proposed for the summer. So I've been thinking, how about if we negotiate an agreement that seems workable and fair to everyone?" We did work out an agreement (see Chapter 8, Negotiating Agreements) and had a great summer. Most importantly, I challenged and overcame a fear and negative emotions that otherwise would have resulted in many more key moments and would have harmed my relationships with my children for years.

On many occasions, it's sufficient to simply think of the steps of Stop–Look–Listen–Choose at a high level—stop the flow of negative emotion; look at the consequences of our current thoughts, feelings, and behavior; listen to our heart whisper what is really important; choose a better way. The process can happen quickly. For persistent and troublesome key moments, it makes sense to take time to review each step and even write down our responses.

## SEEKING SUPPORT

Learning to make strengthening choices is not something we need to do on our own. If we are soft-hearted, there are many people willing to listen and offer their support in our parenting journey. It is often very helpful to have a trusted friend or loved one in whom we can confide our key moments and how we're learning to handle them.

In addition, we may also connect with our higher power (whatever that means for you) in order to find the calmness or strength necessary to handle key moments. For many people, tapping into the grace or loving presence of a higher power helps change their natures so they can become better parents. For many, it is a means for finding the strength necessary to let go of fear, anger, or uncertainty and replace these emotions with clarity, calmness, and inner strength.

Jack accessed this power as he stood outside his son's room and prayed not to change his son but himself. He undoubtedly prayed that his own heart would be changed, his soul enlarged, so he'd have the strength to listen with understanding and not react to the messages of his son.

## MANAGING STRESS

Another aspect of handling key moments is keeping ourselves in a good place emotionally. Sometimes we react poorly during key moments because we're emotionally depleted, our deeper needs aren't being met, or we're experiencing stress in other aspects of our lives. We react, knowing that it's not really about the kids. They're an easy target for venting deeper feelings of dissatisfaction. In addition to developing our awareness and using a technique like Stop–Look–Listen–Choose, we need to pay attention to our general level of well-being. This is particularly important for stay-at-home mothers or primary caregivers who spend so many hours with children, each and every day.

Creating structure, meeting personal needs daily, maintaining a social network, finding sources of success outside of the family, and engaging in spiritual rituals (worship, meditation, prayer, relaxation, yoga) are all practices to help us regenerate emotionally and find balance. If these are missing, then we're much more likely to become depleted and emotionally reactive. So an important part of parenting and learning to handle our key moments includes structuring our lives in ways that enable us to feel deep levels of personal satisfaction. Sometimes doing so requires a lot of creativity and personal responsibility.

## SUMMARY

As stated at the beginning of this chapter, our natural tendencies to overreact are often the biggest obstacles to good parenting. Our kids, young and old, know how to push our buttons, and before we know it, we find ourselves caught up in power struggles or acting in harmful and unproductive ways. However, by becoming aware of our reactions and exercising our agency during a moment of choice, we can learn to parent from a calm and powerful place inside.

CHAPTER 6

# Communicating in Strengthening Ways
# (The HERO Principle)

T HE NATURE AND QUALITY OF relationships define a nurturing family. Relationships, in such a home, are based on values such as love, trust, kindness, respect, and cooperation. These values are expressed through the way we communicate and interact with each other and our children. Communication is the behavior part of the three-part model I introduced in Chapter 3.

Principles ———→ Behaviors ———→ Outcomes

By communication, I'm talking about more than sharing information and coordinating schedules. Communication is how we connect emotionally and spiritually. From our communication we learn about life, make sense of our experience, build relationships, solve problems, express our basic needs, and even have fun together. It is through communication that we relate to, influence, and guide our children.

The purpose of this chapter is to present a model of family communication. The model is made up of the three themes: honesty, empathy, and responsibility. The three themes are an alternative to the weakening patterns of over managing and overindulging our children, particularly during key moments. Here's an overview:

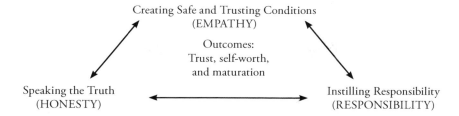

1. **Speaking the Truth** (**honesty**) is disclosing our own feelings or point of view, or giving feedback and getting concerns on the table so we can talk about sensitive topics in a way that helps our children and relationships grow. The intent is to help our children face up to reality, make good decisions, and learn to cooperate with others.

2. **Creating Safe and Trusting Conditions** (**empathy**) is creating an atmosphere of love, empathy, and respect. It lets children know that we value and accept them even though they have weaknesses and make mistakes. Creating such an atmosphere is deeply nourishing and allows our children to feel good about themselves and explore their thoughts and feelings as they learn to make good decisions.

3. **Instilling Responsibility** (**responsibility**) involves skills that teach our children to become self-governing and claim ownership of their lives. They are an alternative to telling, rescuing, or doing for our children what they need to learn to do for themselves. They help children step into the driver's seat of their lives.

There are a number of specific skills associated with each of these three themes, which we'll explore in depth in upcoming chapters. What is important, for now, is to understand the three themes and learn how we continuously "shift gears" from one theme to another, depending upon the flow and desired outcomes of our communication. The themes can be thought of as a toolkit to help us communicate with our children in strengthening ways.

By the way, I call this the HERO principle of parenting.

**H**onesty + **E**mpathy + **R**esponsibility = **O**utcomes

Effective parenting calls forth the hero in each of us. Parenting is not for the faint of heart. It requires courage and integrity to learn to respond rather than react to the key moments that occur almost daily. Although we don't receive medals or public acclaim from others, our day-to-day behavior is heroic because it is not easy and yet it has incredible consequences in the life of a child.

## THE CARLSONS—A DO-OVER

Let me introduce the HERO principle by going back to the example of John Carlson and his parents from Chapter 4. Remember how John's mother reacted to John's grade by overindulging him, telling him that it was okay, and she'd talk to his teacher? John's father reacted by over managing him. He came down hard and imposed some pretty severe consequences on John.

Let's suppose that these parents begin talking and realize that their approaches were not helpful. Fortunately, the Carlsons are soft-hearted enough to know that they need to do something different. So they come up with a different approach and decide to speak to John again. Here's how it might go.

| Theme and Commentary | Dialogue |
|---|---|
| They go down to John's room and knock a few times. | John, brusquely: "What do you want?"<br><br>Mom: "It's your mom and dad. Could we come in?" |

| | |
|---|---|
| Wounded and resentful but also curious, John expects the battle to continue. | John, after a pause: "It's a free country," he states coldly. |
| | John is lying on his bed, face down in a pillow, as his parents come into his room and sit on the edge of his bed. |
| Honesty (disclosure) | Dad: "I came on pretty strong a little earlier, didn't I?" |
| Empathy (listening) | John shrugs. "I guess." |
| | Dad: "That must not have felt good." |
| (Parents are okay with silence) | John is quiet, avoiding eye contact. |
| Empathy | Dad: "You didn't need me yelling at you and giving out all these punishments. That probably made you feel small. You must be pretty mad at me right now." |
| (Parents let John express himself, stifling their own need to defend) | John: "You never listen to my side of things. You always think you know what's best for me." |
| Empathy followed by honesty | Dad: "I can see that. What I don't want is to make it so we can't talk. How about if we start our conversation over again. Would that be okay with you?" |
| | John warily responds: "I guess." |

53

| | |
|---|---|
| Responsibility | Mom: "As your dad and I talked, John, we recognized that your grades are your responsibility, not ours. It doesn't matter what we think. We're curious to know how you're feeling about your F in English." |
| | John: "It's not nearly as big a deal to me as to you." |
| Empathy | Mom: "Uh huh." |
| (It would be easy for parents to want to lecture right now) | John: "Well, it's not like it's the end of the world." |
| | Dad: "True enough." |
| Responsibility | Mom: "Does it concern you?" |
| | John: "I don't like getting an F. But Mrs. Bowman is so unfair. She's treating this class like we're high school or college students. She gives us all this stuff to read and then has us write essays on it in class. It's really dumb. We're only eighth graders." |
| Empathy | Dad: "So you think she expects way too much." |
| | John: "She does. Nobody likes her. Everybody thinks it's stupid." |
| Empathy | Dad: "It's not what you expected from your English class, especially in eighth grade." |
| | John: "No, I hate it." |

Responsibility

Mom: "So let me ask you something. What will happen if it keeps going the way it is now? Will things get better or worse?"

John: "Worse."

Mom: "What might happen?"

John: "I don't know."

Mom: "Think hard."

John: "I guess I could keep failing my assignments."

Mom: "Then what?"

John: "I'd flunk the class."

Mom: "Then what?"

John: "I guess I'd have to take it over again."

Mom: "Is that what you want?"

John: "No."

Mom: "When might you have to take it again?"

John: "This summer?"

Mom: "Yup. What do you think about that?"

John: "I'd hate it! Why do I have to do this dumb English?"

(Mom and Dad listen but also put responsibility back on John)

John complains for a few minutes, with his parents listening and reflecting his feelings.

Mom: "So what do you want? Are you willing to flunk English?"

John: "Not really."

Dad: "Can we help you come up with a plan to improve your grade?"

All three brainstorm several options—doing assignments, asking for help, talking to his teacher, etc., until they come up with a plan.

Responsibility

Dad: "What do you think John? Are things going to get easier or harder as you advance in grade levels?"

John: "Probably harder."

Honesty

Dad: "Reality is that things will sometimes be hard. You're likely to have classes you don't like or teachers you don't like. Agree or disagree?"

John: "Agree."

Dad: "The question is how you'll handle these challenges. Know what I mean?"

John: "I do."

As you can see from the "do-over," John's parents used all three themes. Dad was honest by admitting that he'd come on a little strong. Not only did his honesty keep him internally congruent but also showed vulnerability and his willingness to take responsibility for his behavior. Both Mom and Dad created safe and trusting conditions by listening and expressing empathy toward John. Their listening helped John feel validated. It also made it safe for him to open up. Finally, his parents asked John questions, rather than telling him what to do or solving his problem for him. This helped John think more deeply about what was happening and begin to take responsibility for his school work.

Be aware that this example doesn't cover the range of skills related to honesty, empathy, and responsibility. I'll be presenting four or five skills related to each theme. However, it does demonstrate how the three themes are integral to strengthening communication.

Also know that there is not a single way or "right" way to respond to a particular key moment. Nurturing parents allow themselves the flexibility to employ different skills, depending on the child, the context, and the outcomes they desire. In fact, these parents are able to step back from a momentary interaction and look at the big picture—promoting the growth and development of their children more than simply solving the immediate problem.

## DESIRED OUTCOMES OF OUR COMMUNICATION

I want to suggest four core outcomes of effective communication in parenting: building trust, enhancing self-worth, fostering maturation, and solving the problem. One reason we overreact and get caught up in unproductive battles is that we're overly focused on only one of these outcomes—solving the problem.

However, a narrow focus on solving the problem makes it easy to fall into the trap of trying to force quick solutions and relying on weakening behaviors that harm children and the relationship: lecturing, criticizing, blaming, threatening, bribing, or fixing. These responses not only result in resentment and unproductive power struggles, but they undermine trust, self-worth, and the ability of children to think for themselves and make responsible choices.

Instead, it is helpful for us to pause and gain a larger perspective during key moments. These tense and challenging events are opportunities to interact with our children in ways that will produce powerful long-term outcomes, if we're willing to make building trust, enhancing self-worth, and fostering maturation as important as solving the problem.

## BUILDING TRUST

Trust is the quality of the emotional connection within our relationships. High trust is the recognition by all parties that the relationship is one of mutual respect and goodwill. We know we can count on each other. We feel safe. We can express ourselves openly and honestly without fear of judgment or reprisal. Trust is essential if we are to influence our children in positive ways. Although we can manipulate, control, and coerce them to do what we want, we do so at a high long-term price as our children feel resentment and learn to turn to other sources for support and guidance. Deeper and more important than solving immediate problems is communicating in ways that build and preserve high levels of trust.

## ENHANCING SELF-WORTH

During sensitive conversations, we need to be committed to communicating in ways that build rather than tear down our children's self-worth. A child of low self-worth is subject to many weakening influences within society. He is likely to succumb to peer pressure, give in to the temptations of the moment, and make poor choices compared with a child of high self-worth. Even when being honest and confronting unacceptable behavior, we can do so in ways that preserve self-worth. Accomplishing this outcome requires that we examine our deepest assumptions and core beliefs about our children to make sure that we are sending positive and uplifting messages. All communication between parent and child, but particularly that which occurs during sensitive conversations, has the potential to either preserve and enhance or weaken a child's self-worth.

## FOSTERING MATURATION

It is, once again, helpful to use key moments as an opportunity to help children become proactive and develop a greater sense of personal capability and responsibility. We want them to be in the driver's seat of their lives; to recognize themselves as responsible rather than victims of events, circumstances, and other people. We do this as we help them make choices and recognize the consequences of those choices. It is easy to rob children of their responsibility through sympathy and feeling sorry for them, rescuing them from their mistakes, doing for them what they can do for themselves, sheltering them from the consequences of their choices, or controlling their choices and behavior. We may feel better, temporarily, but our child has not learned the valuable lesson of standing on her own two feet and managing her own life.

## SOLVING PROBLEMS

Finally, we use the themes and skills of the HERO model to solve problems. The poor report card, violation of curfew, conflict with friends, or talking back are all problems that need to be addressed and resolved. In fact, the objectives of building trust, enhancing self-worth, and fostering maturation are most often learned as family members face and work through problems together. By working through problems, our children grow in their ability to step up to the challenges of life.

## SUMMARY

Our goal is to learn strategies (behaviors) so we interact with our children in strengthening ways. The three themes of honesty, empathy, and responsibility form the essence of strengthening communication. Improving our communication is being aware of which theme we're using during our parenting conversations. Effective communication is also being aware of shifting back and forth between the themes. And we keep our objectives in mind. In any given conversation, we want to communicate in ways that build trust, enhance self-worth, and foster maturation, in addition to solving the problem. These immediate, conversational outcomes lead to the long-term outcomes of a nurturing family climate.

| Principles ➝ | Behavior ➝ | Outcomes — A nurturing climate in which our children: |
|---|---|---|
| 1. We are the authority in our homes. | | |
| 2. Our children are inherently good, capable, and trustworthy. | Honesty Skills | • Know of their goodness and worth |
| 3. Our children long to feel love and connection. | | • Feel safe enough to talk |
| | | • Delay gratification and tolerate frustration |
| 4. We are responsible "to" but not "for" our children. | Empathy Skills | • Act rather than react |
| 5. Our children are responsible for themselves. | | • Solve problems and make good decisions |
| | | • Set and work toward goals |
| 6. Growth requires effort, even struggle. | Responsibility Skills | • Make and keep commitments |
| 7. Limits and consequences teach wisdom and responsibility. | | • Act from a moral and spiritual compass |
| 8. Successful parenting requires that we grow ourselves first. | | • Respect and cooperate with others |
| 9. We're imperfect (and that's okay). | | |

In the next three chapters, I'll teach you specific communication skills related to the themes of Honesty, Empathy, and Responsibility. Although I use the acronym "HERO," I'll be starting with the empathy skills, followed by the honesty skills, and finally the responsibility skills. This is the order that makes most sense as parents learn and practice the skills.

CHAPTER 7

# Creating Safe and Trusting Conditions
# (Empathy Skills)

CREATING SAFE AND TRUSTING CONDITIONS is the foundation of excellent family relationships. We use this set of skills to create an atmosphere of unconditional love, mutual respect, and acceptance. These skills help people know that they are valued and accepted even though they have weaknesses and make mistakes. Such an atmosphere is deeply nourishing and allows our children to grow and live from their best selves.

As we instill Safe and Trusting Conditions, we're creating a nonreactive atmosphere. We eliminate power struggles. Children feel safe to open up and talk about their problems and concerns as well as their joys and successes. In this way, children develop emotional maturity. They learn to identify and understand the inner world of their thoughts and feelings. Such emotional literacy is not an innate quality. It has to be taught. Children who don't learn this are more likely to act out, give in to peer pressure, or get depressed. Research shows that children who do learn to understand and deal with their emotions are more self-confident, better performers at school, and have healthier social relationships. They learn these skills through positive interactions with us, their parents (Paul A. Graziano, et al, "The Role of Emotional Regulation in Children's Early Academic Success," *Journal of School Psychology*, Vol. 45, Issue 1, February, 2007, pp. 3-19).

I liken the use of these skills to creating a fertile soil that permits a tiny seed to develop into a lovely flower. The soil enables the seed to become the flower by releasing its capacity to grow, even though the capacity is within the seed. Through Safe and Trusting Conditions, a child comes to believe in herself, understand her inner world, develop trust in others, and find the courage to open up to the world and engage in a process of exploration and mastery.

There are four primary skills that enable this to happen.

## RESPECTING

Respecting is an attitude more than a communication technique. It is recognition of the inherent goodness and capability of each family member. This does not mean that our children always act from their best selves. We are all imperfect and make mistakes. We sometimes act in negative, destructive, and selfish ways. The skill of respecting is not condoning such behavior. However, it is the ability to see beneath the surface of the behavior to the intrinsic worth and capability of a child. It is seeing him as a human being rather than an object. We can look into his eyes and relate to him with decency and humanness.

We communicate respect in many different ways—through our words, body language, attentiveness, giving of our time, and ability to hear them out. One way is joining a child in their world. This is sitting on the floor with a toddler and letting him direct the play. We set aside our own agenda to be "with" the child without the need to direct, control, or teach. We're in an attentive role. We watch and notice and flow with what he wants us to do. Much of the time, this is simply sitting and watching. As a child becomes a little older, he may direct us in how to play with him. We follow his lead.

As a child gets even older, joining him may include participating in an activity—throwing a ball, coloring, or playing a game on the computer. Again, we're in a conforming mode, willing to take our cues and direction from him.

Talking is a powerful way of showing respect and building our relationship. Of course, we talk every day. But I'm referring to talking that is about connecting in order to know and enjoy one another, the way we might talk to a friend. It doesn't have to be deep. Most of the time it will be chitchat, talking about things that our children are interested in—school, friends, the weather, sports, whatever is up at the moment. We get engaged in such conversations by being curious (not probing) and then listening to what they have to say without giving advice (unless they seek it) or solving problems. Driving in the car or sitting on the edge of the bed as our kids are getting ready for sleep are wonderful times for talking. Such communication helps bind our children to us. These moments deepen our relationships and make it easier for our children to turn to us, rather than peers, for support when things get tough.

We also show respect by allowing imperfection. This means letting go of unrealistic expectations and letting our children be who they are, seeing both their strengths and weaknesses and not believing that it's our job to change them or make them into who we believe they should be.

This reminds me of a teen who was an excellent athlete and pitcher on his high school baseball team. On one occasion he pitched a shutout. Pretty incredible. On the way home, the boy's father tried coaching him about the batters who got on base. Exasperated, the son finally looked at his father and shouted, "Dad, I struck out fifteen batters. Is that not enough for you?" His father replied, "I'm just trying to help. With a little coaching, maybe you'll get all of them next time." The son dropped off the team. How important it is to affirm our children for who they are and what they accomplish rather than criticizing their imperfections.

How often do we fail to respect our children by being embarrassed about or critical of their imperfections? Or how often are we trying to make them over into who we *think* they should be rather than allowing them to be who they are? Allowing imperfection shows deep respect.

Another way of showing respect is letting our children have opinions different from ours. Children, particularly as they get into the teen years, will often share opinions just to get our reaction. They don't believe everything they say, but they're in the process of exploring and coming to a deeper understanding of themselves and life. They have to consider different viewpoints to do so. The worst thing we can do is react, argue, and disagree. More helpful is to hear their opinions, perhaps with curiosity. "I'm curious about this opinion...or how you came to this point of view." "Help me understand your reasoning about this."

This is not a passive posture. It is okay for us to disagree and share our thoughts, or values, as well. But timing is everything! We should do so after we've taken time to understand our child; otherwise the discussion becomes an argument. And we should do so without believing we have to "set our child straight," which only encourages resistance and arguments.

## AFFIRMING

Another form of Creating Safe and Trusting Conditions is affirming. This is communicating love, goodwill, and confidence to children in ways that strengthen or help them feel good about themselves. The communication is not necessarily verbal. Affirming includes touching, hugging, and smiling. In fact, these are the building blocks of trust and positive relations.

Back in the 1940s and '50s Dr. René Spitz (and others) performed a number of experiments with orphaned children. In one study, orphaned infants received little interaction or touch. A nurse would change their diapers and feed them, or care for their physical needs, but otherwise these infants were left on their own.

A second group of orphaned infants were cared for by mothers who were in prison. These mothers were allowed to touch, hold, and cuddle their infants and young children a number of times during the day. Researchers followed both groups for several years and, not surprisingly, found that those who received no touch and affection became severely mentally and emotionally handicapped, suffering from these symptoms for the rest of their lives. On the other hand, those infants who received touch and physical affection grew up to be normal adults, even though raised by mothers in prison (Spitz, R.A., "Hospitalism; A follow-up report on investigation described in volume I, 1945," *The Psychoanalytic Study of the Child*, 2, 1945, pp. 113-117).

This research, which would never be allowed today, demonstrates the crucial role that physical touch and nurturing play in our lives. They are vital if we're to thrive. Although our ability to rationalize our needs increases as we become older, we still have such needs. Most of us crave physical and emotional connection in the form of touch, hugs, and smiles as well as kind, affirming words.

Our children crave this affection. Most youngsters, unless autistic or suffering from some forms of mental disorder, seek it out. They may not as they grow older, but the desire is still present. We need to find times and appropriate age-related ways of providing physical affection at home and in the family so our children don't turn to inappropriate ways of meeting these needs outside the family, such as through inappropriate intimacy with a girlfriend or boyfriend.

Many parents try to do this through tickling. We have to be very careful with this form of physical contact. When being tickled, a child is vulnerable and powerless. A little may be fine, but only taking cues from the child. If or when the child becomes frustrated, we need to stop. Continuing is a form of abuse. Although the child may be laughing on the outside, a natural physiological response, on the inside she may be experiencing deep feelings of vulnerability or powerlessness.

Older children and teens are less likely to seek affection, mostly because they're afraid to seek it out. It might seem "childish." They may be afraid of being rejected by Mom and Dad or of feeling embarrassed or "shamed." They may think it's something they should outgrow. Or they may not seek it due to feelings of resentment toward their parents. In any case, it becomes embarrassing to ask as they get older. Parents need to be sensitive to this and yet continue to extend it to older children through hugs, an arm around the shoulder, a kiss on the cheek, or reaching out and touching a hand, arm, or shoulder. We don't outgrow the need. We become more vulnerable and unable to ask. But receiving physical affection is enormously affirming.

Another way we affirm our children is by smiles and kind words. This is a natural extension of physical affection. Think of the language we use with an infant or baby—"Hey there, you cutie…" "Cutesy, cutesy, cu" (whatever that means). We want to communicate words of endearment with people we love. Such words are incredibly affirming. They touch a wellspring of love and goodwill.

Consider affirmations. These are simple, age-appropriate phrases that build us up and help us feel good about ourselves. Imagine whispering in the ear of a two-year-old, "I love your smile." "I'm so lucky to be your mommy." "I'm glad you're a boy." "It is so fun holding you in my lap."

You wouldn't say the same things to a teenager. It may sound more like: "I love how you do your hair." "It's okay to have your feelings." "It took a great deal of courage for you to stick up for your friend." These are not superficial statements. They require that we "tune in" to our children/teens to know them and understand their world.

Affirming includes being aware of positive behaviors and then commenting on them, not every time but intermittently. "I appreciated you helping your younger brother get ready for church this morning. It helped us have a much calmer morning." "This kitchen is looking so good. Great job!" "I noticed you got right to your homework tonight. That shows lots of initiative." Positive reinforcement, affirming desired behaviors, will do far more to instill appropriate behavior than criticizing or scolding children when they exhibit undesirable behavior.

Affirming may be a compliment or praise about what someone has *done*. But it is also recognizing her *way of being*—the way she has expressed her inner strengths or values through actions she has taken. "I respect your tenacity and courage to continue seeking what is really important to you." This skill is sometimes used when a child doubts their own abilities and we let them know we believe in their strengths, abilities, and resourcefulness. This requires us to see their higher self at a moment they might be unable to do so. Through our affirmations, we empower our children to stand tall and keep growing in meaningful ways.

Notice that the examples above are about a child's effort, actions, and character. Saying, "You're really smart" is not helpful. But saying, "I love how hard you're working on your homework," is helpful. In fact, here are some steps to make affirming meaningful:

1. **Provide it immediately.** The closer the affirmation occurs to the behavior we want to reinforce, the greater the impact and more motivating it will be.
2. **Make it specific.** Specific feedback is more powerful than global feedback. "I love that you fed the dog right on time tonight," is far more effective than saying, "You take such good care of our dog."

3. **Speak enthusiastically.** We need our children to know that we mean it. This is not faint praise, but something we really appreciate.

4. **Include touch.** A touch, perhaps on a hand or shoulder, reinforces the message. The extent of the touch depends on the receptivity of the child. But, as stated earlier, most of our children crave physical contact and affection.

Robert, a ninety-year-old gentleman, recently spoke in a meeting I attended. He told of an incident that happened back in 1933, when he was nine years old. He hurried home from school one particular afternoon and noticed, across an alfalfa field, a car in the family driveway. Wondering who could be visiting, he crossed the field and slipped through the back door of the house and stopped to listen. It seemed that some old friends of his parents had come by for an unexpected visit, people he didn't know. Quietly, he listened to his parents laughing and exchanging stories with the visitors.

Then his father changed the subject. "What time is it?" he asked. "Our son, Robert, should be coming home from school pretty soon. You know, he's the best boy. Only nine years old, but I'm so proud of him. He's such a help around this old farm. He gets home from school and goes out to the pasture to round up the dairy cows without even being asked. He milks them every day without a complaint. He's a good boy."

Robert told of slipping out the back door as quietly as he'd entered, to go start his chores. Only they didn't feel like chores that day, his bosom filled with pride from the words of his father.

Our children need to hear acknowledgments from us, even when—especially when—resentment and ill will permeate the relationship. Affirmations are not faint praise. Nor are they designed to make one feel good momentarily. They are thoughtful statements that reflect either a deeper personal trait, task well done, or effort in completing an assignment. Affirming not only helps our children feel good about themselves but binds them more closely to us.

# LISTENING (AND MIRRORING)

Listening is an incredibly powerful tool in Creating Safe and Trusting Conditions. The skill is so important that I recommend it as the starting point when parents are communicating with their children. Unless a child is clearly out of bounds, we do more to build unity with our children and enable them to take responsibility by using the skill of listening than any other skill.

What is listening? It is suspending judgment and being fully present with another person to understand her experience or point of view. It involves hearing more than the words she is saying by tapping into the deeper meaning, unspoken needs, and feelings being conveyed. It is something that is done with the *heart* as well as the mind.

In order to listen, we need to be willing to avoid many of our natural tendencies—to evaluate, judge, agree, advise, lecture, or interpret. Listening may include stating back what we hear using our own words. More important, however, is setting aside preconceptions in order to fully understand another's point of view. It is used throughout a conversation or at the end to bring closure and review main points and actions. We foster good listening through such simple phrases as:

* Tell me more…
* So you feel…
* Let me see if I understand what you are saying…

Mirroring is a form of listening in which we match a person's emotional state. We consciously imitate the gestures, speech patterns, attitudes, and feelings of another, not in a mocking way, but to get into rapport and create a deep sense of empathy and personal validation. It is something we use most often when a child is upset and expressing a lot of emotion.

Here is an example of the power of listening. In the first example, the father does not listen. Pay attention to the consequences to his young son. Notice the difference in the second version of this story.

## THE SON WHO DOESN'T WANT TO RIDE THE BUS

Brian: "Dad, I'm not riding the bus to school anymore."

Father: "What do you mean you're not riding the bus? How do you plan to get to school?"

Brian: "I'll walk."

Father: "You can't walk. It's too far. Besides, there aren't sidewalks. It's not safe."

Brian: "Well then, I'll ride my bike."

Father: "Brian, you're just not thinking. Do you know how many cars are out on the road at that time of morning? Riding your bike is even more dangerous than walking. I can't let you do that."

Brian: "I know lots of kids who ride their bikes. Their parents don't think it's unsafe."

Father: "Oh, I doubt if it's lots of kids. Besides, you should be happy for parents who love you and are concerned about your safety."

Brian: "Dad, you're not fair. It doesn't ever matter to you what I want. You're always saying no."

Father: "I don't think so. I let you do a lot. Sometimes I think I can never satisfy you kids, no matter how hard I try."

Brian: "Gee, I wish I had never brought this up." (Withdraws, sullen)

Father: "Look, I'll tell you what I'll do. About once a week I'll go into work a little bit later than usual. How about if I drive you to school those days? I know it's not every day, but it seems like a good compromise to me."

How do you think Brian is feeling after this interaction with his father? Is he more or less likely to open up to his father in the future? What was his father's intent? Is he aware of the consequences of his approach on his son?

Let's consider how this interaction might have gone if Brian's father had listened with empathy.

Brian: "Dad, I'm not going to ride the bus to school anymore."

Father: "What's up, son?"

Brian: "Oh, I don't know. Nothing much. I'm just tired of riding the bus every day, that's all."

Father: "You've been riding it a long time."

Brian: "I have. Seven years now, and almost every day. I think it's time for a change. I'd like to either walk or ride my bike."

Father: "So you're exploring other ways you could get to school?"

Brian: "Yeah. It sure would be nice if you could take me. Do you think you could?"

Father: "Well, unfortunately, son, I have to be at work about an hour before you leave for school. I'm not sure that's a very good option."

Brian: "I didn't think so. Maybe I'll have to walk."

Father: "Walking seems like one choice you have."

Brian: "I suppose. The problem is, it's really a long way. I'd have to get up a lot earlier. And besides, we don't have sidewalks, so it's not very safe."

Father: "Walking doesn't seem like a very good option."

Brian: "No, neither does my bicycle."

Father: "It doesn't seem to you that there are any good choices here."

Brian: "Nope." (A long pause and Father is quiet.) "And, you know, it's really not the bus. The bus is pretty convenient. I just don't like the other kids, that's all."

Father: "Hmm. What's going on with the kids?"

Brian: "They're rude and noisy. I try to read or talk to someone, but other kids always interrupt me."

Father: "Sounds pretty frustrating."

Brian: "That's the truth. There's one guy, Blaine. He really gives me a bad time. He's a grade ahead of me and a jerk. I'm the guy on the bus he's decided to pick on. He bugs me all the time by punching me, pushing me around, and calling me names. It's really embarrassing. I dread going to the bus stop; it ruins my whole day."

Father: "It really hurts the way Blaine treats you. It affects everything."

Brian: "Yes. It is ruining school for me this year. It is all I can think about." (Long pause)

Father: "I think sharing this with me took some courage. You didn't know how I'd react."

Brian: "Yeah, but I'm glad I did. I feel better knowing you know."

Father opens his arms and Brian accepts a warm hug. "Maybe we could talk about what you can do about it."

Brian: "I'd like that."

What is different this time around? What is the impact on Brian? On the trust and goodwill within the father-son relationship? On Brian's ability to take more responsibility for his relationships and behavior?

How fortunate that the father avoided the temptation to lecture his son or tell him how to solve the problem. Not only did it build trust and help Brian open up, but they were able to get to the real problem. I call this "bedrock," solid ground. It is getting deep enough to know that we're dealing with real issues. Getting to bedrock requires respect, safety, and openness in our communication. We don't get to bedrock when we don't listen, when we rush in with our solutions.

Of course, this problem is still unresolved. But as I stated in the last chapter, there are other objectives of communication in addition to solving the problem. Consider the impact of this conversation on the trust and goodwill, the son's self-worth, his ability to think through various solutions and take greater responsibility for his problem.

Sometimes our children open up and share a problem that requires us to intervene. Bullying is such an example. This situation requires that the father help his son solve this problem by talking to other adults—the bus driver, teacher, and perhaps principal.

## MEAN BROTHER

Here is another example of listening. The mother of two boys hears screaming from the bedroom and walks into the room to find fourteen-year-old David on top of ten-year-old William. William is really hurting. Mother reproves David by saying, "Stop! Get off your brother right now. To your room, immediately." (See Chapter 8—Reproving Skill.)

Mother takes a few minutes to cool down and decide how to handle David. She then walks into his room. "We need to talk about what just happened with William."

David: "We don't need to talk about it. You're always picking on me and think everything is my fault. Why don't you ever get mad at William?"

Mother: "You might be right that I don't entirely understand your point of view, David. I'm willing to listen to understand. But I also need you to know that what happened is not okay, and we do need to talk about it so it doesn't happen again. So tell me your point of view about what happened this morning." *(A natural reaction would be to immediately start lecturing David. "You're bigger than him. Why do you have to be so mean? I get tired of talking to you about this." And so on. Instead, she decides to listen.)*

David: "William has been bugging me all morning. He pulls faces at me all during breakfast and then stands outside my door and makes these obnoxious noises and then runs away. I tell him to stop and he doesn't. He sneaks back and does it again. I can't stand it."

Mother: "Sounds pretty irritating."

David: "It is. I tried to ignore him, like you tell me, but he just kept coming back. I told him to knock it off, but he wouldn't. He just kept bugging me. He's just this little jerk. You and Dad don't see that. You think he's wonderful. He can't do anything wrong, and I'm the one always getting in trouble. It's not fair."

Mother: "You think we always take William's side. We see him as all good and wonderful even though he can be a jerk to you."

David: "Yeah. You do."

Mother: "What else does he do that bugs you or gets you in trouble?"

David: "I don't know. He doesn't even have to do anything. You and Dad are always laughing at him. You think he's so cute and funny all the time."

Mother: "He gets a lot of attention from us."

David: "And I always get in trouble."

Mother: "How's that?"

David: "You think that everything that happens with William is my fault. And you're never happy with anything I do. The grades I bring home are never enough. You always compare me to Megan. Okay, so she's a straight A student and I'm not. I can't help it. Nothing I do is as good as Megan or as cute as William."

Mother: "So you don't think that your dad and I are as happy with you as with your older sister and younger brother. Is that right?"

David: "It seems that way to me."

Mother: "Come here, young man. I'm sorry if I've given you that impression. Here's what I really love about you..." (Mother uses affirming statements with David.) "So I want you to tell me how I can be more supportive in the future." (They talk about this for a few minutes, with David coming up with a number of ideas. Mom lets David know which of these she can do.)

Mother: "We still need to talk about what happens with William. Can you and I brainstorm a plan so you have some other options rather than beating him up when he's bugging you?"

David: "Okay."


The mother clearly saw David as the problem at the beginning of this conversation. It would have been easy for her to lecture or punish David for mistreating his brother. But by listening, they got to deeper bedrock. She came away seeing the problem in a new way, realizing that David had his point of view as well as William. Her responses helped build trust with David at an age in which he was beginning to pull away from his parents.


## MELTDOWN

Here's another example of listening that also demonstrates the power of mirroring. Eight-year-old Billy has spent the last forty-five minutes building a tower out of Tinkertoys. He brings his mom into his room to show it off, and his four-year-old brother, Henri, dashes up, grabs a piece, and the whole thing comes tumbling down. Billy lets out a bloodcurdling screech and shoves his brother to the floor. What's a mom to do with two screaming boys, one keen on making a human sacrifice of the other?

Mom steps between her boys and tells Henri to go to his room and that she'll come and visit him in a minute. She shuffles a crying Henri out of Billy's room and closes the door, ignoring his protestations. She turns to Billy and mirrors his frustration. "How disappointing that you worked so hard for so long on this beautiful tower and your brother ruined it."

Billy wails even louder. "I spent all afternoon making this. It was the best ever. I'll never be able to make another one like it."

Mom: "It is so frustrating when you work so hard and feel so proud of something and it is destroyed in an instant."

Billy: "Yeah. I wanted to show Dad and now I can't."

Mom: "What a disappointment."

Billy: "And that little brat always comes into my room and messes up my things. He's always doing that."

Mom: "You're really mad at him right now."

Billy: "Yeah. He's so mean."

Mom's mirroring is more than words. Her entire demeanor, gestures, and tone communicate empathy. As she listens in this way, Billy feels heard and validated. His angry feelings run their course and he begins to calm down. After a few moments of silence, Mom asks, "So what do you want to do now?" Billy tells Mom he's tired of the Tinkertoys and is going to go see if his friend Jeff is home.

How easy it would have been for Billy's mother to overreact emotionally by either yelling at him, "Listen to me. This is no big deal. You're making a mountain out of a mole hill. You've built a hundred towers. Stop crying RIGHT NOW!" (over managing), or soothing him by making promises. "It's okay. We can make another tower. Your dad and I talked about buying you some more Tinkertoys anyway. Maybe you and I can go to the store later this week" (overindulging). Instead she supported Billy by mirroring his emotions, trusting the value of letting him express himself, and allowing him to learn to manage his emotions.

As Mom leaves Billy's room, she almost steps on Henri, still lying in the hallway, whimpering. She walks to his room and turns back. "Come here," she says. Henri gets up and follows. "Your brother is very mad at you right now."

Henri: "I just wanted to touch it. I didn't know it would break. He didn't have to hit me."

Mom: "It did break. What do you think about that?"

Henri shrugs.

Mom: "I'm going downstairs to clean up lunch." She turns and walks out of the room.

Although Mom believed that Henri's act was rather innocent, she didn't want to offer him undue sympathy or attention. She'd had enough of the drama triangle—Henri playing victim of his older siblings (the persecutors in this drama) with Mom or Dad stepping in to rescue him. Not a healthy dynamic. Mom wanted Henri to learn from the natural consequences of what happened with his brother.

Listening is not only used to discuss big problems but as a skill we can use during brief conversations as well. Here are a few examples.

Mary: "Johnny is so mean."

Parent: "Sounds like you're pretty upset with him."

Mary: "I am. He came into my room and called Jenny (her playmate) names."

Parent: "That sure didn't seem nice."

Mary: "I'm going to tell his friends that he's a big jerk."

Parent: "You're so mad you'd like to get even."

Mary: "Yes."

Parent: "You'd like to hurt him in the same way he hurt you."

Mary: "Yes."

That is it. Much of the time it's simply enough to show empathy rather than overreact or try to make everything all better. Sure there are times we need to intervene. But we do so too often. A good listening response validates our children but without taking on too much responsibility. There may be a better time to talk to Mary about her relationship with Johnny.

Here's another example.

Child: "I'm bored."

Parent: "You're just not sure what to do right now."

Child: "No. There's nothing fun to do around here, if I can't get on the computer."

Parent: "Yeah, that's got to be a real bummer."

Notice again how easy it would be to slip into giving advice or taking on too much responsibility to solve this problem. The more we do, the more our children let us do and the less responsible they become for themselves. Good listening validates and leaves responsibility where it belongs.

This is not to say that we cannot or should not sometimes help our children solve their problems. But this is best done after Creating Safe and Trusting Conditions and listening. We'll often move from listening into a problem-solving skill like harnessing harmful behavior or asking valuing questions (next chapters). Even these problem-solving skills keep responsibility where it belongs, on our children.

I want to summarize the value of listening by sharing a quote from a philosopher by the name of Thich Nhat Hanh. He said:

*When we are mindful, we notice that another person suffers. The other person may be a husband, wife, or child. If one person suffers, that person needs to talk to get relief. We have to offer them our presence by listening deeply… That is the practice of love—deep listening. But if we are full of anger, irritation, and prejudices, we don't have the capacity to listen to the people we love. If people we love cannot communicate with us, they will suffer more. Learning how to listen deeply is our responsibility. We are motivated by the desire to relieve suffering. That is why we listen. We need to listen with all our heart, without intention to judge, condemn, or criticize. And if we listen in that way for one hour we are practicing true love. We don't have to say anything. We just have to listen… When we are in contact with another's suffering, a feeling of compassion is born in us. Compassion means to "suffer with."*

There may be no greater gift we can give our children than to listen deeply.

# SUPPORTING

Supporting is the final empathy skill. This is putting aside our own concerns and asking "What do you need or want?" "How can I help or support you?" It is a skill that often follows naturally from listening and is an alternative to giving advice or trying to fix the situation. It places responsibility on a child to let us, as parents, know how we can be helpful. We need to be careful when we use this approach so that we don't weaken others by taking on too much responsibility or doing for them what they need to do for themselves (e.g., a parent who writes a report for a child). Our support is playing a helping or secondary role.

Notice how supporting could be used in some of the previous examples. John Carlson's parents could and did ask: "John, how can we support you in your studies and grades?" Brian's father could ask, "What can I do to support you, Brian? How can I be of most help to you?" Likewise, David's mother can ask, perhaps after they talk about what David can do to respond to his brother's teasing, "What role do you need me to play as you work this out with William?"

# SUMMARY

I started with the empathy skills because they are so positive. They are the foundation of a nurturing home and means by which we build strong, healthy relationships with our children so that we can both enjoy *and* influence them, today and for years to come. Of course, these skills require that we believe in our children. It is impossible to use these skills if we don't trust their goodness and capability. But if we can believe in them, then we can use these skills to help them feel their worth and empower them with responsibility to think deeply, make better decisions, and become self-governing.

# RESPECTING

See goodness and uniqueness of a child
 * Take time
 * Join them in their world

- Talk (chitchat) about what is important to them
- Allow them to be imperfect
- Value them for who they are
- Let them have their opinions

## AFFIRMING

Communicate love and goodwill

- Touch, hug, smile (nonverbal love)
- Tell them you love them
- Comment on the behaviors you appreciate and want to reinforce
- Acknowledge a quality of being or task well done

## LISTENING

Suspend judgment and tendency to react; be present to understand child's experience/point of view

- Tell me more...
- So you feel...
- Let me see if I understand...

## SUPPORTING

Ask, rather than guessing or taking over

- What do you need?
- How can I support you?

# CHAPTER 8

# Speaking the Truth
# (Honesty Skills)

S PEAKING THE TRUTH IS BEING honest about our feelings and perceptions in order to help ourselves, children, or relationships grow. The skills are used to disclose feelings and perceptions, share feedback, or talk about conflicts and sensitive topics with compassion and forthrightness.

A difference between the honesty versus empathy skills is that *we* (as opposed to the child) are instigating the communication. We, as parents, have a concern about something that we need to get out on the table.

Some of the honesty skills that you'll be learning in this chapter are "soft," whereas others are quite confrontational. More important than the particular skill we are using is our intent. Although honesty is often spoken plainly and boldly, it should always come from a loving heart and not simply to give vent to our feelings.

Speaking the Truth is not easy. It requires self-awareness, congruence, and compassion. We need to be mindful of our timing and use the skills when we are not reactive and when we sense that there is an openness and readiness on the part of others. It is wise to sometimes delay using one of these skills until our hearts are soft and in a better place.

## GOALS OF SPEAKING THE TRUTH

There are two goals in using the honesty skills. First, they must strengthen our children. The skills help our children become more aware, learn to manage their emotions, become better problem solvers, and learn how to cooperate with others.

The second goal is to honor and take care of ourselves. We honor *others* as we practice the skills of Creating Safe and Trusting Conditions or empathy. We honor ourselves as we practice the skills of Speaking the Truth. We use these skills to express our own feelings and needs, set boundaries, and teach others how to treat us.

Children need to be taught to be concerned about others. After all, they begin life self-centered. A baby cries and we feed her, change her diaper, hold and comfort her. Life is all about me, me, me. Very literally, a child, in her mind, is the center of the universe. However, as a child grows older, she develops more autonomy, including the ability to take care of her own needs. But she will continue to be quite self-centered and demanding unless taught that others also have needs and feelings and a point of view different from her own. We teach our children respect and cooperation (rather than always getting their own way) as we use the honesty skills.

There are many ways of Speaking the Truth—disclosing our feelings, telling someone what we want, sharing our values and what is important to us, giving feedback, letting someone know what we'll accept or not accept. In the remainder of this chapter, I want to present five specific honesty skills which we can learn to use to strengthen our children and take care of our own needs within our parent-children relationships.

## DISCLOSING

Disclosing is getting our thoughts and feelings into the open so our children don't have to guess or remain in the dark about what is going on inside of us. Think of disclosing as sharing information not readily observable or "knowable" by others, but which matters to us and may also affect our relationship. Disclosure may be positive ("My heart is full of gratitude toward you") or negative ("I am frustrated that whatever I do never seems to be enough"). The purpose is not to control (although some of the skills establish clear boundaries around what is/is not okay) but rather to provide children information to expand their awareness, learn how to get along with others, and make better choices. Here are a few examples:

"These are my feelings about what is going on..."
"Here's my point of view..."
"This is what I believe and why..."
"This is what is important to me..."
"Here is how this situation affects me..."

Good disclosing is an "I" message rather than a blaming message. This means that we take ownership of our perceptions and feelings rather than attributing the cause to someone or something else. Rather than "You make me angry," we say, "I feel mad when such and such happens." We own our experience.

Because disclosure is an "I" message, it is expressed as a point of view rather than a dogmatic statement (the whole truth and final word on the subject) that doesn't allow for the point of view of others. Such statements are communicated in a clear, even bold, and yet respectful way that allows our children to make up their own minds or make their own decisions.

Remember the example of a father talking to his son who didn't want to go to church. Rather than launching into a lengthy lecture about why his son should be in church, the father shared his own experience. "I go because I love to feel the Spirit. There's something, at least for me, about participating in a holy ordinance that is a touching experience..." Such a disclosure is far more powerful than telling a teenage son what he should think, feel, or do. It is personal and meaningful and yet shows respect and displays trust in his son's ability to think and decide for himself.

Another example of disclosure is John Carlson's father's confession as he and his wife got their chance at a do-over with John. He said, "I came on a little strong earlier, didn't I? You didn't need me yelling at you and giving you a lot of commands."

Hear the softness. Hear the ownership. Hear the truth. This is disclosure. The intent is not to manipulate, but to share information in a way that allows our children to understand, see, or feel differently.

Much of our disclosure is sharing our positive feelings, which we so often keep to ourselves. This reminds me of a story about a twelve-year-old boy who looked up at his father, walking into the house after a long day, and said, "I love you." His father stared at his son, at a loss for words, waiting for the other shoe to drop. *He must need help with his homework* was the father's first thought. Or, *He's going to ask for an advance on his allowance.* Or, *He's assassinated his brother.* The first words out of the father's mouth were, "What do you want?"

His son laughed and started to run out of the room when his father called him back. The boy, grinning, told his father that his health teacher had given the class an assignment to tell their parents they loved them and see what would happen.

The next day this father called the teacher to find out more about the experiment and learn how other parents were reacting. "Most of the fathers had the same reaction as you," the teacher said. When she first asked the kids to try the experiment, the students laughed. A couple of them figured their parents would have heart attacks.

The teacher explained that feeling loved is an important part of health and something that all human beings require. She reported that she was trying to teach kids that it's important to express their feelings.

Well, this father thought about those words. When his son came to him that evening to say good night, the father held onto him for an extra few seconds. Just before his son pulled away, the father said, "I love you too." He went on to say that perhaps next time one of his kids came to him and said "I love you," it wouldn't take him a full day to think of the right answer. (D.L. Stewart, "Hey Son, I Love You Too," from Jack Canfield, et al. *Chicken Soup for the Parent's Soul,* [Health Communications, Inc., Deerfield Beach, FL, 2000] p. 90).

So often our positive feelings are unspoken. I think of my kids as I write these words. What are the feelings that are deepest in my heart that I so often fail to say to them? What would I want to say, if I had a little more courage?

What is deepest in your heart? What edifying message do you want your children to hear from you?

Disclosure may also be used when feelings or perceptions are negative. A mother comes home from a day of work only to find the house a cluttered mess. She could go on a rampage and shout orders. (Maybe if she's been over indulgent for too long, insisting on action wouldn't be a bad option.) Or per-haps she opts for disclosing. She might walk up to her oldest and say some-thing like, "Charlotte, it is utterly disheartening to me when I come home to a cluttered mess. I want to go to my room and have a good cry." That's it. She may walk away and get on with the evening routine, knowing that she may need to circle back at a more convenient time to establish expectations or negotiate agreements and consequences.

Many disclosing statements, when feelings are negative, consist of three parts: "When you...I feel...because..." For example, "When you don't come home by curfew, I feel sick with worry because I love you so much and don't want anything bad to happen to you." Or, "When you bicker with your broth-er, I feel so sad because two of the people I love most are not getting along."

Disclosures don't always include all three parts, nor are the parts always delivered in the same order. The important thing to remember is to keep the focus on the impact of the child's behavior on us. This helps them think more deeply and understand the consequences of their behavior.

One final comment about disclosing negative feelings. It is sometimes very appropriate to express our anger as part of disclosure when a child's be-havior is clearly disrespectful or violates our needs and feelings. It is okay to say, "I feel angry when I ask you three times to do a chore, because you don't seem to care about doing your part around the house." Or, "It frustrates me when you interrupt me when I'm on the phone, because it doesn't show re-spect to me or the person I'm talking to."

We have feelings and needs just as real as those of our children. We don't help our children if we don't teach them respect. They need to learn to become aware of others and deal with the realities of living in an interpersonal world.

Disclosing is one of the "soft" honesty skills. It's not always sufficient to shape our children's behavior. It is just one tool. But it does deepen the communication and help our children become more aware of what others think and feel. It does so in a respectful way that avoids resistance and power struggles.

## CARE-FRONTING

Care-fronting is the second honesty skill. It is giving frank and honest feedback to our children about behavior that is either outside their awareness, harmful to others, or interferes with our needs as parents. Whereas disclosure is revealing our own inner experience, care-fronting is giving information about our children's behavior. The feedback is information that can potentially alter or reshape a child's perceptions, behavior, or way of being and thereby lead her to grow or take more effective action. These messages are succinct and well timed in order to affect a shift in the receiver. They are often expressed in the form of an observation and consequences:

"What I see happening is…" and "The consequences I see are…"

Such messages must always be delivered with respect and care and never when we are so upset that we can't communicate in a respectful way.

My father used this skill with me when I was fourteen or fifteen. Three of my friends had been over on a Saturday afternoon and we'd been playing basketball on the driveway. After they left, my father approached me. "Roger, can I share something I noticed about you and your friends?" Curious, I agreed. "I noticed you making yourself the brunt of jokes. You put yourself down a lot. Are you aware of that?" His feedback surprised me. It made me think about our interactions and I recognized it was true. I remember him going on to say, "Your friends like you. In fact, this isn't something they do to you. You do it to yourself."

I remember this experience because it had an impact on me. Although something I was doing, it had been unconscious. The feedback made me aware and caused me to change the way I was acting and communicating with my friends. I recognize, looking back, that I'd played a bit of the clown and even the fool to get attention. I liked the laughs, but my father helped me recognize the harm it was doing to me.

I recall using this skill when I taught a youth Sunday school class. I was twenty and the students were juniors and seniors in high school. I thoroughly enjoyed the class and we got along great. The twenty or so students were lively, active, and engaged, making the class fun. However, one student, Mark, did not know when to be serious. The self-proclaimed "Steve Martin" of the group, he was always making jokes, sometimes to the disruption of the class. As a good-looking and popular kid, he got away with a lot.

One day I pulled Mark aside and the two of us took a walk down the hallway. I said, "Mark, I love having you in my class. I enjoy your personality and humor. However, there are times when I feel it is disruptive. It keeps me from teaching my lesson and you and your friends from learning, which is why we are here. Do you know what I mean?" (Here is what I see happening… Here are the consequences…)

Mark hemmed and hawed a bit and told me that he didn't mean anything by his jokes. It was his sense of humor. I listened and then told him that I didn't want to take this good trait from him. I went on to tell him that he would have to decide the role he'd play in a group, not just our class but other groups as well. I challenged him: "Will you use your personality and natural leadership to contribute positively to what is happening around you and help people grow and become better? Or will you use it negatively, leading people to be less than they can be? That decision is yours and not I or anyone else can make it for you. But I do want to ask, as long as you are in my class, that you show respect to me and the others by being serious at the appropriate times and participating in our discussion. Will you do that?"

Mark looked down. After about five seconds of silence he said, "Yes, I can do that." Mark was appropriate after that incident. His behavior changed and he became a positive influence on other class members and a pleasure to teach. Of course, the class members graduated from high school and went their separate ways. I did not hear again from Mark. Then one evening, about twenty years later, my wife attended a speech given to a youth group. The speaker came up to her afterward and said, "Hi, my name is Mark." He told her about the incident when he was a seventeen-year-old high school student. He said the incident caused him to reflect on his behavior and its consequences, and he had made a decision to change. He wanted my wife to let me know that confronting him had awakened him and made a difference.

I've still not met Mark as an adult, but the experience was another reminder to me of the difference we can make by care-fronting, especially when done with an attitude of respect and goodwill.

This skill works best when we speak from a loving heart. In other words, our intent cannot be to punish or demean, but to edify. The purpose of using the skill is not only to stop a harmful behavior but to do so in a way that contributes to the growth of the individual.

Care-fronting statements are usually brief and informational. Otherwise, they become preachy and our children will tune us out.

Although we may make a request at the end of the observation/consequences statements, it isn't always necessary. Sometimes we simply leave the individual with the feedback and give them the emotional space to process it. It is important to leave the responsibility on the child. By saying too much we take the responsibility away from the child.

Like so many of the skills, don't expect a quick fix. Much of what we're doing through our communication is planting seeds. As we interact with our children in new ways, we're changing ourselves, not them. As we change, they will change, but not always immediately.

## Reproving

There are times when honesty needs to be more confrontational. A child is acting out or his behavior is clearly inappropriate, and softer methods of communication have not worked. The skill is based on the same principles as care-fronting but is spoken with greater boldness and firmness.

Here are examples of behaviors when we might use this skill.

* Sassing or blatant disrespect
* Not following your directions (son continues to play Xbox when time is up; or we have to call a child to the table several times)
* Hitting siblings
* Cursing

Notice that in each of these examples, the child is acting in a clearly inappropriate way. The skill is used to communicate a limit (what is appropriate and not appropriate) and correct behavior that is out of bounds. Here are the steps:

1. **Give a clear (even sharp), usually one-sentence correction.** We don't want to be too wordy. This is not about moralizing, lecturing, or justifying our point of view, but letting them know what we will not accept or tolerate. ("It is *not okay* to not come when I call.")
2. **Ask or tell them their next step.** Sometimes we ask them what they can do to correct the behavior. More often we tell them exactly what we expect them to do. ("Come. Now.")
3. **Disengage.** This may be mental or physical, depending on the situation. Sometimes we walk away. If not, we turn our attention away from the child so we don't get caught up in an argument or explanations. We look away or continue what we were doing, *expecting* them to comply.
4. **If they fail to comply, impose a consequence.** If the child does not comply, don't go into arguing, lecturing, or threatening. Carry out a consequence related to the behavior. They may go to a time-out, lose a privilege, etc. (See Chapter 9, Enforcing Consequences.)
5. **Show love afterward.** It is always good to circle back and show love to the person we have reproved. This is a time to show softness, to ask a few questions, to invite our child to talk about what happened, to reinforce not only our limit but our love. The caution is that we can't do this too quickly or we undo the effect of our reproof.

For example: Five-year-old Michael hits his three-year-old brother with a toy car. His mother saw what happened and walks over to Michael and states, sternly, but without yelling. "You do *not* hit your brother, *ever*. Hitting is not okay in this house. Now leave the car and walk away from your brother." Mother immediately turns and walks from the family room to the kitchen, expecting that he'll heed her message. A few seconds later Michael falls to the ground crying. Mom ignores him and continues preparing dinner, knowing she'll go back to comfort him in a few minutes.

Ten-year-old Sally is doing her hair. Because she's going to be late for school, her mother comes over to help. Sally shouts, "Get out of here. Leave me alone." She hits her mother with her brush. Sally's mother kneels in front of her. "It is never okay for you to shout or hit. Now give me the brush." Sally shoves it into her mother's hand. Her mother continues brushing her hair, with Sally crying. Mother says nothing more before school. That evening she takes some time to listen to Sally talk about her day.

Notice a few characteristics about using the reproving skill. The behavior is occurring in the moment and is clearly inappropriate. We deal with the behavior and not with emotions or justifications for the behavior. In other words, this is not a time for sensitivity or empathy. Our purpose is to set a limit by letting our child know, emphatically, that the behavior she displayed is not appropriate and will not be tolerated. The skill requires that we act from authority. We have to be firm but calm. Once we have compliance, we let go of the issue. We can't punish, lecture, or hold a grudge after the incident is over. Finally, this is a skill that should be used infrequently and usually with younger children.

A younger child who has been reproved will sometimes cry. His crying is an act of submission, allowing us to be the authority and accepting our limit. Crying is also a way for a child to express and even soothe his hurt feelings or painful emotions. It's a natural process that we should allow. This doesn't mean we're unsympathetic. It means we're willing to allow the child to feel and deal with the emotion of being corrected.

Of course, if we let go of the issue as soon as it is over, then we're able to interact with our child from goodwill and not resentment or hostility. The child will sense this and know that our "harsh" intervention was not a comment about his worth but rather about a behavior that was not appropriate.

## NEGOTIATING AGREEMENTS

Negotiating Agreements is an honesty skill to resolve conflict. The intent is to find solutions that meet the needs of all family members, parents and children alike. The process of letting children participate in making agreements helps them mature. They learn to think about possibilities and consequences. They learn how to engage in dialogue, the importance of give-and-take, and the necessity of cooperation. And certainly one of the great benefits from using this skill is "ownership." Children who have a part in making agreements view them as "their" agreements, not arbitrary rules imposed by Mom and Dad.

In the traditional, authoritarian model, parents impose their will on their children. "This is how it's going to be." There is a place for this, particularly if the family structure has been lax or children have been overindulged and feel entitled. We sometimes need to take the lead and establish clear boundaries or rules. But generally children won't learn responsibility or internalize good values if we unilaterally make decisions for them.

By the time children are in elementary school, they should be allowed to negotiate some agreements. They can help decide, for example, when they'll do homework versus go outside and play. They can help decide what chores they'll do and when they'll do them, or which extra activities they'll participate in (piano, soccer, dance) and how they'll show responsibility for these activities.

As children become teenagers, they will be taking on more responsibility and showing greater autonomy in their decision making. They will determine much of what they do. We encourage this as parents. However, sometimes their decisions affect us or the rest of the family. These become opportunities to negotiate agreements.

As parents, we take the initiative and guide the negotiating process. We do this by raising concerns, bringing the right people together, getting different perspectives and feelings on the table, and then searching for solutions that everyone can agree upon.

Let me share an example. In Chapter 5 I told the story of our oldest daughter refusing to accept our daily schedule for the summer (see page 46). My point, in that chapter, was to illustrate how I used Stop–Look–Listen–Choose to change myself so I could become a more effective parent. However, the story didn't end because I got myself into a better place emotionally. My wife and I still had to talk to our kids about our summer routine. Here is the rest of the story.

At our next family council we taught our kids the following four-step process for negotiating agreements:

1.  **Get all points of view on the table.** The intent of this step is to create a common understanding before we try to solve the problem. Therefore, it's essential that we not judge or criticize one another's point of view. Everyone gets a chance to talk. Each person can talk more than once.
    *   "This is how I view the situation..."
    *   "How do you view the situation?"
    *   Continue until all feelings and points of view are out on the table.
2.  **Identify what is most important to each person.** This is not the same as a solution. What is important is deeper than a solution and becomes the criteria by which we measure solutions.
3.  **Brainstorm various solutions.** We don't judge any ideas but put them all on paper. We want all possible solutions to take into account what is important to each person.
4.  **Agree upon our final solutions.** Our final solutions are selected from the brainstorming list above. They have to be solutions that we can all agree upon.

So we began with step one. What do you guys think? What is your point of view? The kids shared things like, "We've been in school and need a break." "It's not fair for you to tell us when we have to get up." "We want to decide our schedule during the summer." Judy and I listened. We reflected back what we heard to make sure we understood.

Then we took our turn stating our point of view. "You're going to have a break and lots of free time." "There are still chores that need to be done." "Summer isn't a free ride. You have some responsibilities." "Having fun is important." "Discipline and routine are good."

We then moved on to step two. I asked, "What is most important to you guys this summer?" We heard: "We need a break." "We want to have fun." "We want to have some say in what we do and how we do it."

Judy and I shared what was important to us. "We want you to enjoy your summer." "We want some structure and discipline." "Everyone needs to help with the chores so it isn't all up to Mother."

Step three. We brainstormed various solutions. The rule was no criticizing. We wrote all responses.

* Kids do chores by 8:00
* Kids decide when to do their chores
* Chores must be done every day
* Dad does all chores (this one got a chorus of cheers)
* Breakfast served by 8:00
* People get own breakfast
* Clean up after self
* Dinner together

Step four. We accepted only the solutions we could all agree with.

* Kids decide when to do their chores
* Chores must be done every day
* People get own breakfast
* Clean up after self
* Dinner together

The evening felt like a win-win, and the summer turned out well. Our children cooperated and did their part. Perhaps more important, I learned that I needed to communicate differently with my children as they grew up. I could no longer decide for them but needed to involve them in coming up with the agreements that would govern our family life.

Here is another example of negotiating agreements. Our son Jon was a junior in high school. I picked him up from school on a Friday afternoon, and we began talking as we drove home. He told me he wasn't feeling well. He was tired and had a sore throat. Then he reminded me of his regional track meet the next day, which would last most of the day.

Me: "Should you really go, Jon?"

Jon: "I can't miss it, not just for me but for my team. I can't let them down."

Me: "I understand, but you're sick. You won't do the team much good if you're sick."

Jon: "I'll be okay. I've got to go."

Me: "It's your call. I just get worried when you tell me you don't feel well."

Jon: "Yeah, and I have this big report due in science next week. It's worth 30 percent of my grade."

Me: "Oh wow. How's it coming?"

Jon: "I haven't started it."

Me: "You've got to be kidding."

Jon: "Nope. It won't be that hard. I'll get it done."

Me: "When will you work on it?"

Jon: "I'd better get started this weekend. It's not due until Tuesday, but I'm not going to have time to do the whole thing on Monday night."

After dinner, Jon spent some time in his room. I hoped he was working on his science project. Unfortunately, when I went to his room around 8:00, he was lying on his bed, listening to music. We talked a little. Of course, I wanted to ask him why he wasn't working on the project, but knew it was his responsibility, so I left. I came away feeling greater anxiety about his health and how he was going to get everything done over the weekend.

The next day we went to the track meet. It was a pretty long, hot day. Jon did okay but not the greatest times. I could see he didn't feel well. We came home and he disappeared. An hour or so later he came to me. "Dad, I want to go to Mike's tonight. He's getting a group of kids together and we're going to play some games and then go TP Megan's house a little later."

That was it for me. "No way, Jon." I launched into a lecture. "You complained about not feeling well yesterday. You've been away all day in a track meet. You have a huge project due at school next week, and besides that you haven't even done your chores yet. No, you can't go."

Needless to say, he was upset. I went up to our bedroom and closed the door because I didn't want to be around him. Before long, I heard him doing his chores, vacuuming and then mopping the kitchen floor. I could hear commotion including doors and cupboards slamming. He was letting me know he didn't like my answer.

I decided we'd better talk. I went downstairs to his bedroom, knocked on the door, and waited for him to invite me in. "Jon, let's talk about what is happening right now between you and me. I get that you're pretty upset. I have this little four-step process which can help us resolve this conflict between us. You game?"

Jon: "I guess."

Me: "This is negotiating agreements. We've done it before." I briefly reviewed the four steps and then said, "You start. Step one is to tell me how you see the situation."

Jon: "You're being very unfair. I'm sixteen years old and ought to be able to make a decision like that. You're being mean and controlling."

Me: "So I'm not being fair or sensitive to your needs."

Jon: "Yeah. You don't live my life. You don't know how I feel or my schedule for getting things done. I ought to be able to make my own decisions."

Me: "It doesn't seem fair when I step in and tell you how things should be."

Jon: "Right. I talked to Mike today and he has this great party planned. And I miss most things like this because I have to get up so early for my paper route. I'm really looking forward to this."

Me: "It sounds like lots of fun, and you don't get to do things like this all that often."

Jon: "Yeah."

Me: "Can I tell you how I see it?"

Jon: "I guess."

Me: "Remember when I picked you up from school on Friday. You told me how bad you felt. You told me about your track meet all day today and then the project you have to get done by Tuesday. All of that made me concerned and worried, mostly about your health but also about your school work."

Jon: "But it's *my* school work."

Me: "Hey. I get that. I did a good job of listening to your point of view. Now I want you to understand my point of view. I know it's different than yours, okay?"

Jon: "Okay."

Me: "So everything you shared with me made me very concerned about you. Then when you came and asked to go to Mike's, I couldn't believe it. I was already worried. It seemed to me too much for you to stay out late, not only because you have complained about not feeling well, but because of this big project. I'm thinking, when is he going to get it done, if not tonight?"

Jon: "But it isn't your decision."

Me: "I understand. Hey, I'm just explaining how I see things, Jon. That's all. This is how I see the situation. We see it differently. See what I mean?"

Jon: "I guess."

Me: "Okay, let's go to step two. Can you tell me what is important to you?"

Jon: "Well, it's important to me to make my own decisions. I don't like it when you tell me what to do. I'm too old for that."

Me: "Okay." Then I continued, "I'd like to jot this down," and went and got a notebook and pencil. "What else is important to you?"

Jon, after thinking for a moment: "It's important to have some fun. I feel like I have a lot of responsibility. I've always got something that I can do—work or homework or my chores, something. I need to have some fun with my friends."

Me: "Got it. What else?"

Jon: "That's really it."

Me: "Well, let me share what's important to me. It's important to me that you take care of your health and get over this cold and sore throat."

Jon: "Okay."

Me: "It's important to me that you get school work done. Ah…it's important to me that you and I talk when we are upset with each other. That we not go to our rooms but that we really talk to each other about what is going on and come up with a solution."

Jon: "Yeah."

Me: "Okay. Now let's brainstorm solutions. Let's not judge any of the solutions but just list them and then we can go back and choose which will work best for both of us."

Here's the list we came up with.

1. Jon goes to party tonight and Dad says no more about it.
2. Jon doesn't go to party but stays home and works on project.
3. Jon doesn't go to party and is in bed early.
4. Jon works on project between now and when it's time to go to party.
5. Jon figures out a schedule of how long it will take to do the project and shows it to Dad.
6. Jon goes to party but comes home at midnight. He doesn't go TPing.
7. Dad goes to party with Jon.
8. Jon gets some good sleep between now and Monday morning. This can include tonight, Sunday nap, and Sunday night.

Me: "So here's the last step, Jon. Let's pick some options from this list that we can both feel good about, that feel like a win for both of us."

Here are the final agreements we could both support:

#4. Jon works on project between now and when it's time to go to party.

#5. Jon figures out a schedule of how long it will take to do the project and shows it to Dad.

#8. Jon gets some good sleep between now and Monday morning. This can include tonight, Sunday nap, and Sunday night.

I didn't get everything I would have liked during this conversation. Heck, I would have preferred Jon stay home and work on his project all evening. Furthermore, Jon's agreements were not enforceable by me. However, this process was not about me imposing my will, which only breeds resentment and power struggles. It was about coming up with solutions that we could both support.

In addition to coming up with agreements, there are a number of secondary benefits from going through this kind of conversation. We're learning to talk. We're building trust and goodwill. I'm staying connected to my son but without being overly controlling. I'm helping Jon learn responsibility by thinking through choices and consequences.

Some people tell me that negotiating agreements takes too much time. I get that. But I also say, "Pay now or pay later." I'm saving time down the road as we learn to communicate. We're building a deeper relationship so we don't get caught up in the wrangles that go on between many teens and their parents. By taking time up front, I'm saving time in the future and teaching my son valuable lessons in getting along with others.

There are many situations that may call for negotiating agreements. A child comes home from school each day and wants to immediately go outside and play. We're concerned about her doing her homework. So we sit down and do some negotiating. Or a son wants to spend every spare moment playing computer games. Or a son buys a mini-bike and has been riding it places he should not. Or, a popular daughter is starting to date and you need to talk about a curfew.

Let me point out that not everything is negotiable. As parents, we have the right to set limits within our homes. As I've stated elsewhere, this is particularly important for young children or when parents have been overly permissive and need to assert their authority. However, if we want our children to become self-governing and learn skills in communicating and collaborating with others, then we need to allow them to participate in creating the agreements by which they will govern themselves. This is especially true as they get older.

In each of the above instances, there were other skills that we could use with our children. I could have just listened and supported Jon. I could have used the care-fronting skill to give him feedback and then let him make his own choices. I could have set some limits by letting him know I wouldn't permit him to go. Which skill we use is a judgment call. It is not right or wrong. In fact, nurturing parents give themselves flexibility to test and try different methods and do what works.


# HARNESSING HARMFUL BEHAVIOR (ADAPTED FROM WWW.EMPOWERINGPARENTS.COM)

Some children are compliant; they listen and follow authority. Others are strong-willed, or even defiant, more likely to act out their feelings and fail to listen and follow direction. Defiant children are more difficult to parent, and we have to parent them somewhat differently than compliant children. We employ the skill of Harnessing Harmful Behavior to deal with challenging and strong-willed children or any child who is acting in a belligerent and harmful way.

Jack is an example of a strong-willed teenager. He turns requests from his parents into big productions. He argues every time they want him to do chores and claims that they pick on him. Easily frustrated, he yells or throws things when he doesn't get his way.

These children aren't bad. The problem is that they use poor strategies to solve their problems. Their strategies are an immature way to solve their problems and almost always hook their parents into either arguing with them or giving in. Here are some of their most well-used strategies:

1. **Victim stance**. They play the victim and try to get us to believe that they were innocent in what happened. If they stick to their story, they won't be held accountable.

2. **Blame and excuses.** It's never their fault. It is always about what someone else or some situation has done to them.

3. **"It's not fair."** They continually see things as unfair, justifying their failure to follow the rules. They put us on the defensive by making unfairness the focus instead of dealing with their own unacceptable behavior.

4. **"You don't understand."** They want us to believe that not understanding them is the problem and not their behavior.

5. **Anger**. They train us to give them what they want by being angry or losing control. Their emotional outbursts cause us to back down, giving them power and control. We're afraid to trigger them and so we don't deal straight.

6. **Avoidance**. They don't see that they have to do work to meet a goal. They avoid or resist goals and commitments and put off what they don't want to do at the moment. If we push them, they revert to anger.

All children use such strategies at times. The difference is that defiant children become masters of them and use them whenever things aren't going their way. Again, they don't use them because they are bad, but because they lack the ability to deal with their emotions and solve their problems in more mature ways.

The first step in dealing with difficult children (or any child being difficult in the moment) is to notice the strategies and stop giving them power. Our awareness allows us to see them for what they are so we can stop being hooked. We're then free to communicate in more effective ways.

Once we can see their strategies for what they are and can stop being hooked, we can focus on a better goal—that of helping them learn more appropriate strategies for managing their emotions and solving their problems. That isn't what most of us have been doing. We've been trying to survive and bring an end to the drama. We haven't seen that the child's lack of maturity is the underlying problem. That should be our goal, help them become more mature.

Harnessing Harmful Behavior can help us accomplish this goal. It is a skill to bring a child face-to-face with the harmful consequences of his behavior and teach him to solve problems rather than act out. To harness means to control power or energy for a productive purpose. We harness a horse not to kill its spirit but to channel and use its energy in productive ways. That is also true of children. We don't want to stifle their spirits or diminish their passion, but want to make sure it is directed in positive ways.

So here are the steps in Harnessing Harmful Behavior. The process is used either during or following an incident in which our child is acting out or has acted out.

1. **Initiate a conversation.**
2. **Invite child to share his point of view about what happened.** Be a good listener. Note his use of responsibility-avoiding strategies (from the previous list), but don't comment at this time.
3. **Place responsibility by asking questions.** Although there are many variations, the questions generally sound like:
   a) What was the trigger to your reaction? (The purpose of this question is not to justify the reaction but help him become

aware of the external events that trigger him so he can watch for them in the future. Remember, we are helping him learn from the event that has taken place.)

b) What choices did you make? (Keep him focused on what he and not others did. We may need to redirect a few times. "I hear what your brother did. I'm asking you to talk about the choices *you* made.")

c) What are the consequences of your choices? Is this what you want?

4. **Process faulty thinking**. We do this during step three. Every time we hear our child use faulty thinking or a strategy to avoid responsibility (victim, blame, "not fair," etc.), we calmly but firmly "call" him on it. Here are three ways we do this:

d. Sidestep these strategies by staying focused on the questions. "Nevertheless, what choices did *you* make?" "I understand you think this is unfair, but what did you do that wasn't helpful?"

e. Challenge the strategy directly. "You aren't a victim. You made choices."

f. State that whatever was going on does not justify inappropriate behavior. "Being upset with your brother doesn't mean you can yell at the family."

Don't get sidetracked from your agenda of helping the child look at his choices and take his responsibility. Keep coming back to the questions.

5. **Create a plan.** Ask your child what he can do next time this occurs. Help him develop a plan by thinking through different alternatives and then select what will work best. The plan should be in his own words and be okay with us. Make sure it is realistic and concrete: "I'll ask for help when I get stuck with math." "I'll tell my sister that I want to be left alone and will leave if she keeps bugging me."

6. **Reward good behavior**. Determine, together, a reward for the next time he follows his plan rather than acting out. It should be something concrete and motivating to the child. Make sure you provide the reward when he does the good behavior.

Let's apply these steps to a real situation. A teenage son gets mad easily and yells at other members of the family. Such an incident occurred last night and we now want to talk to our son, using the Harnessing skill.

Dad: "Josh, we need to talk about the incident last night when you got mad and started cursing and throwing things around the living room."

Josh: "I don't want to talk about it. It's over."

Dad: "It's not over. As a matter of fact, everyone has been walking on eggshells since then. What happened was a big problem and we need to talk. Josh, look at me for a moment. My purpose in talking to you about this is not to blame and punish you. It's to help you learn a better way of dealing with your frustrations, other than swearing and calling people names."

Josh: "Well, I still don't want to talk about it."

Dad: "I'm not willing to let something like this slide. Not talking is not an option. We will talk about it. If you refuse to talk now, then no more Wii or TV until we've talked. Your choice."

Josh: "Oh. I guess. I just hate this."

Dad: "So, help me understand what happened. What was going on when you got so mad?" *(Dad's purpose really is to understand and to help Josh begin to understand what triggers him as well as his emotional reactions and their consequences.)*

Josh: "I don't know. I was playing on the Wii and Kelly kept bugging me. She kept saying it was her turn. But it wasn't. She kept trying to take my joy stick when I was in the middle of a game and it really ticked me off. She wouldn't back off. So I got mad. Then you and Mom always take her side. You didn't know what was going on."

Dad: "Okay, Josh. I appreciate hearing your point of view. Now I'm going to ask you some questions. My purpose is not to make you defensive but to help you learn some new ways of dealing with situations like this. What choices did you make that contributed to what was going on?"

Josh: "It wasn't me. It was Kelly. This wouldn't have happened if she didn't keep bugging me."

Dad: "Josh. You were there. It was you who got mad. You may not have liked what Kelly was doing, but you had choices about how to handle what was going on."

Josh: "Why do you always blame me? Why aren't you talking to Kelly? She started it!"

Dad: "I'm not talking to Kelly because I'm talking to you. This talk is not about blaming you. It is about helping you make better choices when you get upset. So, let's talk about your choices. What did you do when this started happening?"

Josh: "It's not fair. You always pick on me. I'm the one who always gets in trouble around here, not the other kids."

*(Dad has a decision to make. Is this an avoidance strategy? Is there some truth to it? When do you deal with it, now or at a later time? Dad decides that what is important, now, is harnessing this behavior. He can circle back and listen to Josh's concerns after they've addressed this problem.)* "Listen, Josh, you're not cooperating with me. Everything you say is to avoid dealing with this issue, which I'm not willing to do. Let's talk now, or we can talk later and you'll lose the Wii and TV in the meantime."

Josh: "Well, what do you want me to say?"

Dad: "Be honest. Don't avoid your responsibility here. What did you do that contributed to this problem with Kelly?"

Josh: "Well, I kept playing when Kelly wanted me to give her the control."

Dad: "Okay. What else? How did you talk?"

Josh: "I yelled at her."

Dad: "What was the consequence of that?"

Josh: "She got mad and tried to take it from me."

Dad: "Then what did you do? What choice did you make?"

Josh: "I said 'no' and kept playing. I wasn't going to give it to her when she was being mean."

Dad: "How'd that go over?"

Josh: "Not good."

Dad: "Were things getting better or worse, Josh?"

Josh: "Worse, I guess."

Dad: "Is that what you want?"

Josh: "Well, Kelly needs to back off and be more patient."

Dad: "Josh. You're blaming again. It is very easy for you to tell me what Kelly should be doing. And I'll be talking to Kelly. But right now I'm talking to you. Is this what you want?"

Josh: "I guess not."

Dad: "What do you want?"

Josh: "I want her to not bug me."

Dad: "Can you control her?"

Josh: "No."

Dad: "What can you control?"

Josh: "Me, I guess."

Dad: "I know that what happened wasn't fun for you. You really didn't like Kelly bugging you. We're having this talk to find a better way to deal with things like this. Whether Kelly was right or not isn't the issue. You're always going to have people who bug you and make you mad. The thing is, how will you deal with it? Can you see that?"

Josh: "Yes. I guess so."

Dad: "You and Kelly will have to learn to work things out. I can help you with that. But what is not okay with me is for you to totally lose it and start yelling, cursing, and calling people names. That isn't the kind of climate I want in our home. Know what I mean?"

Josh: "Yeah."

Dad: "So, let's talk about what you can do when something like this happens again. And you and I both know it will happen again, right?"

Josh: "Right."

Dad: "What can you do?"

Josh: "It would be good if Kelly was more patient."

Dad: "Josh. Who am I talking to?"

Josh: "Me."

Dad: "So what can *you* do? You're a smart kid. Go ahead and brainstorm some options here and then you can choose the best. If you get stuck, I'll help you."

Long pause. Dad waits.

Josh: "I could put the control on pause and then look at her and tell her not to bug me."

Dad: "Would that work?"

Josh: "I don't know. Not completely."

Dad: "I think that is an excellent start. Now you are talking to her instead of just reacting. How can you tell her in a way that she'll listen?"

Josh: "I don't know.

Dad: "I'm thinking it might be helpful for her to know what's going on in your head at that point. She isn't sure she'll ever get the control, so she bugs you more. And, by the way, sometimes that happens. You keep it and don't let other people play. What do you say about that?"

Josh: "I guess. Once in a while. But I was planning on giving it to her."

Dad: "Okay. So what else might you do?"

Josh: "Tell her."

Dad: "That sounds really good. So, how can you do that?"

Josh: "When she starts bugging me, I'll hit the pause button and tell her how much longer it will take before her turn."

Dad: "Great. You're really thinking this through. And how do you think she'll likely react?"

Josh: "I don't know. Hopefully, she'll wait her turn. But she might say something mean."

Dad: "And what would you do?"

Josh: "I'll ignore her."

Dad: "Will that work?"

Josh: "No."

Dad: "So what else might you do?"

Josh, after a moment of thought: "I'll tell her that I want to be fair and cooperate. I really will give her a turn."

Dad: "That is excellent, Josh. And if she just persists?"

Josh: "I can walk away and come back later."

Dad: "This is really good problem solving, Josh. You're starting to see that you have lots of choices."

Josh: "I guess so. But I really think you need to talk to her."

Dad: "Maybe. But you can't always depend on others treating you the way you want. You have to figure out what choices you have when things aren't going your way. Know what I mean?"

Josh: "I think so."

Dad: "This is very good. I'm proud of you, son. I think we should think about a good reward when you do this. Let's come up with something that would be a real incentive to you, when you're in the heat of the moment, to carry out your plan."

Father and son brainstorm and decide that Josh will get an extra hour of time on the Wii as a reward. They agree this won't happen all the time, just the next time Josh handles a problem with Kelly in a good way.

Here are some guidelines for using Harnessing. Notice that the goal is not to punish the child or even just stop harmful behavior. The purpose is to help him learn better ways of dealing with his emotions and solving problems, including handling conflicts with others. The issue, in this situation, is not about sharing a remote. It's about Josh learning that there are better choices than blowing up and yelling when things don't go his way.

Harnessing Harmful Behavior requires that we use our authority. Although it is best if our heart, as a parent, is soft, it is certainly not a soft skill. It requires a very active role on our part in order to ask choice-consequence-related questions and "call" a child on his responsibility-avoiding strategies. But that parental authority has to be used in a calm way that allows us to be connected to the child.

Notice how Josh's father insisted that they talk about the incident. He was not willing to let it slide, for Josh's sake as well as the rest of the family. However, it's often best not to talk during or right after an incident. It's usually better following a cooling-off period. It's even okay to negotiate a time to come back together.

Of course, we can't force a child to talk. If he refuses then we impose a consequence. It has to be something the child really values as well as something we can enforce. We let our child know that the consequence will be lifted as soon as we have our conversation. A deeply resentful child may accept the consequence rather than talk. That has to be okay or we'll give the child power to defy and punish us. Our attitude has to be "And that's okay with me."

A final thought about this skill. We need to be willing to listen to genuine concerns expressed by a child. We may learn something about his deeper resentments or fears that we can help resolve. However, we can't allow these to divert us from searching for a solution to this problem. We can always make a mental note and come back later to ask about his concerns.

## SUMMARY OF HONESTY SKILLS

We use the honesty skills for two reasons. First, they are a means by which we give our children information to help them become more aware, learn to manage their emotions, solve problems, and cooperate with others. The skills teach them to think more deeply about their behavior and its consequences and decide what is in their best interest.

Second, and equally important, these skills are the means by which we take care of our own needs. We have needs too. Relationships are two-way. Through our honesty we honor ourselves by letting our children know what they can and cannot do in our relationship. Not only does this make our time with our children more pleasant, but it teaches them skills in empathy and respect.

## DISCLOSING

This is what is important to me...
This is what I believe and why...
What do you think?

## CARE-FRONTING

This is what I see happening...
Here are the consequences I see...

## REPROVING

1. Give clear (even sharp) correction
2. Ask (or tell) next step
3. Disengage
4. If failure to comply, impose consequence
5. Show love afterward

## NEGOTIATING AGREEMENTS

1. Develop a common understanding of perceptions/feelings of each person
2. Discover what is important to each person
3. Brainstorm various solutions
4. Agree upon final solutions

## HARNESSING HARMFUL BEHAVIOR

1. Initiate conversation
2. Invite child to share point of view
3. Place responsibility with questions
4. Process copouts (victim, blame, etc.)
5. Jointly create a plan
6. Determine reward

# CHAPTER 9

# Instilling Responsibility
# (Responsibility Skills)

THE TOPIC OF PERSONAL RESPONSIBILITY has been a core theme through-out this book and is the centerline on the pathway of maturation. I think of it as much more than completing a task or doing our duty. At its heart is our right and ability to make choices at all times and in all circumstances. Responsibility is strapping ourselves into the driver's seat of life; knowing that we choose our thoughts, attitudes, and actions; learning to act proactively, rather than being acted upon by circumstances and events. Ultimately, it's the knowledge that we create our destiny through our ability to choose.

As we internalize this principle, we grow in our ability to:

- Make good choices/decisions
- Delay gratification and tolerate frustration
- Accept accountability when things go wrong
- Make and keep commitments
- Act from a moral and spiritual compass

This process is not about perfection but rather maturation. We can't force responsibility (just like we can't make a flower blossom). Instead, we can learn to interact and communicate with our children in ways that encourage their development.

As loving parents we sometimes unintentionally do things that prevent our children from developing responsibility. Out of fear or not knowing a better way, we fall into the traps of over managing and overindulging our children in ways that prevent them from taking full responsibility for their lives. We impose from without rather than helping them develop responsibility from within.

The purpose of this chapter is to introduce a number of skills to help our children take responsibility.

## CREATING STRUCTURE

By structure I'm talking about routines, expectations, and mechanisms that define the rhythm of family and shape individual behavior. Mealtime, bedtime, chores, play, worship, family prayer, and holiday traditions are examples of structure. These repeatable patterns make up the culture of a family and also become ways in which we influence and teach our children valuable life lessons, including responsibility.

We need routines and traditions. They create order and make our world predictable. They also teach us how to behave and get along with others. Although parents will differ about how much structure they want within their family, structure is critical to all families. Young children, particularly, do well when they follow a predictable, albeit flexible, routine.

My wife Judy and I created quite a bit of structure when our children were toddlers and elementary school-age children. Breakfast was ready at a certain time each morning, and the kids had to dress and make their beds before they could eat. Not unlike those of other families, their routine included going to the library or shopping on certain days of the week as well as a quiet time in the afternoon, in which everyone stayed in their bedrooms, either napping or playing by themselves. We had dinner together as a family and a bedtime ritual that included gathering together to sing, read scriptures and a book, and pray.

As our children started kindergarten, we bought each one an alarm clock. That was pretty exciting to a five-year-old. We taught them to use it and expected them to get themselves out of bed and ready for school every morning. Getting up at the sound of the alarm, dressing, and being ready for breakfast were all mechanisms and routines to help them learn responsibility.

Star or earnings charts are another form of structure that some families use with their children. Such mechanisms create expectations and direct the focus of children on the most important behaviors they need to accomplish during the day. Stars or points reward them for appropriate behaviors—getting up on time, making their beds, doing homework, cooperating, and completing chores. Although the rewards are external, children learn and internalize good behaviors. Such structures help children develop good habits and make them responsible for managing their lives. (See example of an earnings chart in Appendix G, page 153.)

Of course as children get older, the routines and expectations change. Their responsibilities become greater. By the time our children were in elementary school, we had created another structure—a budget. At first it was simple. You earn money from doing these chores. Ten percent is put aside for charitable donations. Forty percent is put into a savings account. Fifty percent can be used to buy things. However, we had rules about how they could spend this money. It wasn't okay to bring their money every time we went to the store. We would talk to them about something they wanted, usually in the ten- to twenty-dollar range, and then they would save their money until they had enough to make the purchase. This structure helped them take responsibility for their money and taught them the relationship between their efforts and rewards.

When they were teenagers, their budgets became even more important. We paid them so much per week, as long as they completed all their chores, but also made them responsible for *all* of their expenses—clothing, school supplies, entertainment, everything. They had to live on this money. If they needed a pair of jeans or shoes, they'd buy them. If they wanted to go to a movie or eat lunch with friends, they'd pay. They couldn't come to Judy and me and ask for money. We'd buy them gifts at Christmas and one nice gift at their birthdays, but otherwise, they were on their own.

If they blew it and spent too much on a gift for a friend, or toy they wanted, okay. That was their decision, but we weren't going to bail them out because they were broke. "Better luck next time." It didn't take them long to learn that making a lunch or eating in the school cafeteria was a lot cheaper than eating at a restaurant.

Their allowance was never enough to pay all of their expenses, so they had to work. They all got jobs—babysitting, delivering newspapers, mowing lawns, doing odd jobs for Mom—so they could have more money. As they got older, they could work at fast-food restaurants, retail stores, or car washes. They learned the value of work and the relationship between their efforts and rewards.

Chores are another important part of family structure. These change, of course, as children get older, but children at most any age can and should do work around the house or yard. Little ones need help and someone working alongside them. But they naturally love to help Mom or Dad knead bread, sort laundry, pick up toys, make beds, or even do dishes. Letting them participate in household chores helps children begin to value the importance of work and understand that everyone contributes to the family.

Sometimes it's easier to do certain jobs by ourselves rather than involve our children. That may be true. But the goal is more than a clean house or nice meals. It is also the development of our children. If we wait on them when they are young, they expect it when they are older. They aren't learning the discipline of work or the importance of their responsibilities to family members.

So it is important to see the relationship between family structure (routines, expectations, and physical mechanisms) and the ability of our children to learn responsibility. Structure elicits certain behaviors from family members. Children learn that there are ways we do things. Everyone participates and everyone contributes. They learn how to behave and give back to the family.

## ENFORCING CONSEQUENCES

Closely related to creating structure is the skill of setting limits and enforcing consequences. In the real world, there is a cause-effect relationship between our choices and their consequences. If we don't go to work, we don't get a paycheck. If we don't put oil in the car, the engine freezes up. If we don't feed the dog, it will die. We may not always like what we have to do to get certain consequences (getting up at 5:00 a.m. to go to work), but we value the consequences (paycheck and sense of contribution) and so we're willing to do hard or inconvenient tasks.

## NATURAL CONSEQUENCES

Our children also have to learn this lesson. They have to experience the *natural consequences* of their behavior so they can begin to develop the discipline and wisdom to make good, even hard choices. Some choices don't require special action on our part. We step back and trust our children's ability to learn from their experience. They won't always make good choices, which is how they learn. A child who doesn't eat goes hungry. One who goes outside without a coat gets cold. Forget an assignment and get marked down. The teenager who refuses to study for a test gets a poor grade. An adolescent who runs out of gas walks home.

The challenge is to let reality be the mediating agent. If our children are accustomed to us intervening, coaxing and persuading, rescuing, and doing what they are capable of doing for themselves, then they learn to make unwise choices. They haven't yet learned the cause-effect relationship between their choices and the subsequent consequences. They're more caught up in the "game" and power struggle going on with their parents. We need to give them space to experience the natural consequences of their decisions.

## THE VALUE OF "NO"

Perhaps the simplest and earliest limit our children learn is "No." This is one way we set boundaries and let our children learn and accept the realities of life. "No" can mean "I don't want you tearing pages out of books," "I'm not buying candy at the store," "I don't want you hanging all over me," or "You can't go out with friends tonight."

If a child wants something badly, hearing "No" results in frustration and disappointment. Consequently, children (from toddlers to teens) will whine and fuss or throw a tantrum when they don't get what they want. However, if it goes on and on it's because they've learned that if they keep whining and throwing fits, they'll wear us down and eventually get what they want. We reward our kids for fussing. We're afraid to say "No" because we don't want them to be upset with us or we don't want them to be sad and disappointed. So we give in or get caught up in trying to convince them that "No" is for their own good. We take too much responsibility to keep them happy by over-negotiating everything they want. By so doing, we create an unpleasant home environment, one that wears on us.

If we try to prevent disappointment, our children become self-centered and entitled. They also fail to learn responsibility for their emotions and inner experience. When a child has to deal with a "No" in its many forms, she learns to handle sadness and disappointment. She learns to soothe herself instead of expecting life to always give her what she wants. After all, life doesn't grant us every wish and whim. We mature as we learn to tolerate disappointment and frustration.

So we need to say "No" and not get hooked into feeling like a bad parent or feeling sorry for our children. They'll not only handle "No," they'll grow emotionally mature and look back, one day, and see the wisdom of our parenting.


## LOGICAL CONSEQUENCES

Sometimes our children need more than "No" or even natural consequences. As parents, we have expectations and have to impose *logical* consequences on our children when they fail to abide by the norms of family life. We don't do our kids a favor when we have no expectations or fail to enforce limits. In fact, we're teaching them that they're not accountable. They can behave poorly, be lazy or disrespectful, and there won't be consequences. Such children are slow to become self-governing or responsible. They learn to play the victim, get others to rescue them, or seek the pathway of least resistance.

I believe in the V principle of parenting. This means that we impose more limits and consequences when children are young and then become more flexible around many limits as our children get older and need to learn to choose for themselves. When children learn about rules and consequences at a young age, they learn valuable lessons in trust, respect, and personal responsibility which they naturally carry with them into adolescence and adulthood.

Let me give you a simple example. I recall our daughter Cheryl-Lynn, at age eighteen months, continuously dropping her food on the floor. Her mom and I let her know that it wasn't okay and if she continued she'd be removed from her high chair. Of course, a few minutes later she smiled at us as she dropped food off her tray again.

Without a word, I picked her up, carried her upstairs to her bedroom, put her in her crib, and closed the door. I was just a few steps away when I heard, "Whaah, whaah, whaah." Judy and I chuckled but kept eating. After five or so minutes she stopped crying. She was standing in her crib and reached for me as soon as I entered her room. I took her down the stairs and placed her in her high chair with the words, "If you throw your food on the floor, I'll take you to your room again." The rest of the meal was fine. She got the message.

So often we tend to talk rather than act. Cheryl-Lynn drops her food and we say something like, "Cheryl-Lynn, leave your food on the tray, not on the floor." She smiles and does it again. "I'm serious, Cheryl-Lynn. Please don't drop your food on the floor." I look away and before long more food is on the floor. "Cheryl-Lynn, NO! You don't throw your food on the floor. If you keep doing it, I'm going to get you down."

By now it's a game. Cheryl-Lynn is getting lots of attention and having fun seeing me react. She is feeling and testing her newfound power. After pleading some more, I'm likely to grab her and angrily march up to her bedroom. "This is not okay. How many times do I have to tell you?" And then when I bring her back down, we go through the same scenario again.

The key to enforcing limits is taking *action* rather than getting upset, talking, nagging, pleading, lecturing, or bribing. Action, not words, teaches children to be responsible for their behavior. It allows them to learn from reality rather than forcing them to comply. It helps them become inner directed rather than outer directed as they recognize their own choice making is central to the consequence.

Here are the steps of Enforcing Consequences:

1. **Know your expectations/boundaries.** Most expectations have to do with conformity to family routines, personal conduct, responsibilities for helping out. These won't be the same in every family. More important than where we draw boundaries is that we ensure they are clear and that we enforce them consistently.

2. **We must accept our authority and parental power.** This is hard for many parents who want to please their children or keep them happy all the time (impossible and not our job). Many parents give their authority away in the name of keeping the peace, not wanting to upset their children, or not wanting to do the hard work of enforcing a boundary.

3. **Allow or follow through with a consequence** (action) when an expectation is violated rather than over-parenting by lecturing, threatening, reminding, or rescuing. It's easy to end up talking about the violation instead of taking action.

4. **Our follow-through of the consequence must be:**
   - Immediate
   - Consistent
   - Without hostility
   - Without guilt

I like the analogy of gravity. If I trip and fall, the consequence is immediate and consistent. Gravity doesn't get mad. Nor does it feel sorry for me. The consequence is matter-of-fact. We teach responsibility by allowing or imposing consequences in the same way.

Children who don't pick up their toys lose those toys and have to earn them back. A child who doesn't come to the table when called doesn't get to eat. A child who gets up late and misses the bus has to pay Mom to drive him to school. A child who doesn't eat dinner doesn't get dessert. A child who pitches a fit in a store is taken home, perhaps immediately, and doesn't go with Mom next time. A teenager who damages the car can't drive again until he pays for the damage. A teen "forgets" to do her chores, and Mother "forgets" to wash her clothes. A teen who flunks a class isn't able to play video games in the evening until he can demonstrate the steps he's taking to improve his grade.

As parents, we make enforcing limits too complicated. We want our children to comply, but we don't want to enforce consequences, so we end up doing all sorts of weakening behaviors like ordering, threatening, bribing… all in the same conversation. The problem is that we're trying to change the child (which we can't control) rather than our own behavior (which we can). Children learn that we aren't serious and so they ignore us or have fun watching us go through all sorts of psychological gyrations to get them to do what we want. They get all sorts of payoffs out of this behavior. Initially, it's inconvenient to enforce boundaries. However, long term, family life becomes more peaceful and productive. Pay now or pay later.

It helps to think through good consequences ahead of time. In addition to allowing natural consequences, logical consequences need to matter to our children and be enforceable by us. Here are some examples of enforceable consequences: going to bed early, losing TV/computer or screen time, doing additional chores, paying for lost or broken items, going to their room, losing out on a fun activity, losing a toy, cell phone, or the car.

Although many consequences are natural and easy to determine, there are times when we're really not sure what to do. It is okay, in such instances, to take some time to figure it out. This is far better than meting out arbitrary or unenforceable consequences. Once we've come up with an appropriate consequence, we can apply it consistently, without guilt or hostility.

A friend was having a difficult time getting her nine-year-old daughter to practice the piano for fifteen minutes every evening, something they'd discussed and agreed upon at the beginning of the school year. Mother and daughter were caught up in a power struggle, and the daughter was winning. The mother was feeling increasingly frustrated and powerless.

She sought my opinion, and we talked about who owned responsibility for practicing the piano. The mother agreed it was her daughter's responsibility. "Can you let her take this responsibility?" I asked.

"But how?" she asked, telling me it would never happen without constant reminders.

"Stop reminding, coaxing, and nagging," was my reply. "Let her be responsible and see how she handles it. If she fails to practice, then she doesn't get to do something (a privilege) that she really loves."

Of course, if our children are accustomed to us taking their responsibility, then they'll be slow to pick it up for themselves. So the mother choked back her words as she observed the daughter failing to practice the piano each evening.

Then came Wednesday. The daughter anxiously approached her mother. "Mom, we're going to be late for my dance class!"

"But Stacey, you aren't going today."

"Why not?"

"Because you forgot to practice the piano every day. That's what you have to do to go to dance."

Needless to say, Stacey was pretty unhappy that evening. But her pouting didn't hook her mother, who stuck to her guns. Stacey changed her behavior because she knew that her mother was serious.

## MAKING EXPECTATIONS CLEAR

It is necessary to be very clear about our expectations and consequences (step one of Enforcing Consequences). Otherwise, we end up being wishy-washy, which sets up ongoing battles with our children. Here is an example of a mother who decides to do a better job of clarifying and enforcing expectations.

Playing Xbox has become a problem for thirteen-year-old Michael and eleven-year-old Sam. They stay on way too long and then pitch a fit when Mom finally coaxes them off. So she took some time to clarify her expectations:

- You can play Xbox two nights a week, Tuesday and Thursday, plus Saturday.
- You must complete daily homework and chores before you can play.
- You must set a timer for forty-five minutes on weeknights and ninety minutes on Saturdays.
- Get off immediately and without a fuss when time is up.

She also took some time to think through consequences for failure to comply with these expectations. She came up with the consequence that her boys would not be able to use the Xbox at the next scheduled time. And they'd lose the privilege for a week if they had two incidents during a single week.

She then had a meeting with her boys to communicate her expectations and consequences. She first stated the expectations and then asked her boys to repeat them back so she knew they were clear. It went like this:

Mom: "I've been thinking about your use of the Xbox. It has been causing a real problem lately because you guys have had a hard time getting off and then spend the rest of the night being grumpy and uncooperative. Xbox is a privilege and I want to share what I expect in order for you to continue using it." She then explained the four expectations outlined above and asked, "Michael, what are my expectations for you to use the Xbox?"

Michael: "These are silly rules, Mom. I don't know why I can't spend more time if I've got my homework and chores done. Most kids spend as much time as they like. Their parents aren't as mean as you and Dad."

Mom ignores the negative comments and persists: "Nevertheless, what are our expectations?"

Michael: "Mom, this is dumb."

Mom: "Dumb or not, we're only going to let you use the Xbox if you follow our rules. Otherwise, the Xbox goes away. What are our expectations?"

Michael: "I can't believe how stupid this is. Okay, I have to do my homework and chores before I can play."

Mom: "Very good. You were listening to me. What else?"

Michael: "Oh brother. I hate this. We only get forty-five minutes on weeknights and ninety minutes on Saturdays."

Mom: "Great. Which weekdays can you play?"

Michael, with resentment in his voice: "Tuesdays and Thursdays. You think I'm stupid, Mom?"

Mom: "No. I just want to make sure we are clear. What else do I expect?"

Michael: "I have to get off immediately. But, Mom, that is a really hard rule. If I'm in the middle of a level, I can't just get off; I have to finish."

Mom: "What is the rule?"

Michael: "You don't understand, Mom. You haven't played. You don't know what it's like."

Mom: "What is the rule?"

Michael: "I have to get off immediately."

Mom: "That is exactly right. Very good, Michael."

Notice that Mom did not get sidetracked into arguing with Michael. She ignored his drama and persisted with her agenda, reinforcing him when he stated what she wanted to hear. We have to expect that our children will complain about some of our expectations and try to manipulate us into backing down (a natural part of growing up). They do this through anger, pleading, pouting, or anything that will "hook" us into giving in. But we must trust our authority and continue to be clear and firm.

Let's continue.

Mom: "Okay, guys. There is a consequence if you don't follow these four rules. You lose the privilege of using Xbox the next time it's scheduled. If you fail to follow the rules two times within a week, then you will miss Xbox for a full week." Turning to her other son, "So, Sam, what will happen if you don't comply with these expectations?"

Sam: "You already told us, Mom."

Mom: "I want to make sure you understand. What will happen?"

Sam: "Mom, I know what will happen. I don't have to repeat it. You just told us."

Mom: "True, I just told you. What will happen if you don't comply with these expectations?"

Sam: "Mom. You're treating me like a three-year-old."

Mom: "Nevertheless, what will happen?"

Sam: "We'll miss our turn the next time."

Mom: "Exactly. And what if we have a problem on two occasions?"

Sam: "We'll not get to use it for a week."

Mom: "Very good, Sam. I appreciate you repeating this to me so we have a clear understanding. Thanks, guys."

Again, Mom ignores the push-back. Her boys are expressing frustration and disappointment and also testing to see if she'll back down. If she gets hooked, she'll end up in an unproductive power struggle and lose her ability to enforce consequences. By sticking to her guns, she controls what she can, family structure, and allows her sons to take responsibility for their own feelings and behavior. They'll handle not getting what they want, and learn to tolerate frustration and take responsibility for their emotions in the process.

It is true that Mom is taking a pretty hard line here, because this behavior has been a problem and she has not done a good job of clarifying expectations and enforcing her boundaries in the past. Enforcing boundaries in such a way is a "tough-love" skill. And yet, we can simultaneously establish order in our homes through enforcing consequences *and* use other skills to build a nurturing climate and positive relationships.

I don't necessarily recommend using this method to establish clear expectations in all areas of family life at once. Pick an area that has been a problem and communicate your expectations and consequences in this area. Expand from there, once you have some confidence in your use of this skill.

As stated earlier, consequences work best when imposed at a young age. As our children become teenagers, they need more latitude. We shift from imposing consequences to talking, even negotiating agreements, most importantly around issues of moral agency (the choices they make about how to live their lives). Of course, we still have boundaries or non-negotiables around behaviors that affect all family members—chores, language, and respectful behavior. But teenagers are learning to think for themselves and need room to make their own decisions.

Notice how we use limits and consequences not only to teach our children responsibility but also as a way of taking care of our own needs. Many expectations and limits are designed to help us parents meet our needs for a happy and peaceful life.

## ENCOURAGING AUTONOMY

The famous columnist Anna Quindlen said: *When [my children] were very small I suppose I thought someday they would become who they were because of what I'd done. Now I suspect they simply grew into their true selves because they demanded in a thousand ways that I back off and let them be* ("Goodbye Dr. Spock," *Newsweek*, June 8, 2007).

Encouraging autonomy is allowing children to make decisions and do more for and by themselves as they get older. This isn't always easy, and we want to step in and rescue them, by helping a toddler struggling to climb onto a couch or calling the school to rearrange a schedule for an older child. It's better to allow them the trust and space to work many things out on their own.

One way we encourage autonomy is by allowing our children to make age-appropriate choices. A young child might decide what to wear, or at least choose between options presented by his mother. He may also get to decide which meal he'd like from McDonald's. Perhaps an elementary age child may decide whether to play soccer or gymnastics, or decide whether to study after school or in the evening. A middle schooler is going to naturally have more choices about such things as friends, the kind of music she likes, what she does with her free time, and so on. By the time kids reach high school, they should be making most of their personal decisions. After all, they'll be out on their own in just a few years and need this practice.

There is a language that we use as we help our children make choices. For a young child it might sound like: "What would you like to wear today?" "Do you want to take your bath now or in five minutes?" If a child is fussy, the language of choices might sound like, "Beth, do you want to stop fussing and stay here with us, or keep fussing and go to your room?"

As children get older, the way we talk to them about choices changes. For an older child, we learn to help them think through problems or make decisions by asking questions rather than taking over or giving advice. (More about this as we talk about valuing questions.) Such questions might sound like: "What is most important to you in this situation?" Or, "What are you thinking of doing? How might that work?" Our role is shifting from telling to coaching.

Of course, we aren't passive observers of our children's choice making. It's appropriate to set boundaries based on family values (no dating until sixteen; eat meals together; everyone helps with chores; certain music/media is not allowed in the home).

One observation I want to make is that we can give young children too many choices. The choices appropriate for them are those that directly affect them, not others. I cringe when I hear parents asking children to make choices on behalf of the entire family. "What should we have for dinner tonight?" "Where should we go for summer vacation?" To solicit input is one thing. Participation and collaboration are helpful. But some parents give their children too much say in what happens for the entire family. They end up overindulging their children and working too hard to please them. Giving choices to our kids does not mean we abdicate being the authority in our home.

Another way in which we encourage autonomy is by not giving our children too much or doing for them what they should be able to do for themselves. We are an affluent society and so it is easy to buy material goods or spend lots of money on our children. So often they don't have to work for what they get and come to believe that life is easy or things will be given to them.

I recall sitting at a table with one of the sons of Warren Buffet a few years back. His son spoke to that issue. You'd not have known that his father was one of the wealthiest men on the planet. His son told us that his father did not buy or do too much for his children. Furthermore, he remarked that this had been a blessing to him and his siblings.

I've worked with many wealthy families through the years and have seen how wealth can destroy discipline and ambition. Because we can afford to give our children lots does not mean we should. It is not good for them.

When our son Jon was a junior in high school, he came to us and asked if we'd buy a third car. Unless I was out of town or their mother didn't need a car, they rode the bus to school. Jon was appalled by this family policy. It embarrassed him. Everyone he knew had parents who had either bought them a car or owned three cars so their teenagers had transportation. Jon worked on us for quite a while. At one point, I shared with Judy that his request was not unreasonable. But she reminded me that it's good for the kids to learn to sacrifice and to cooperate on transportation. We told Jon that if he wanted a car, he'd need to buy and maintain it. I recall looking with him in the paper at the price of used cars. We then put pencil to paper to figure out all of the costs of maintaining a car—gas, repairs, insurance.

We let him know that all of these expenses would be his, but that we would support him in buying a car, if that's what he wanted. He was amazed at the expense and said he could pay his share of a year of college for that amount of money so was satisfied with using one of the two family cars when he could, catching a ride to school with a friend, and taking the bus as a last resort.

Judy and I were surprised when Jon came to us about the time he graduated from college to thank us for not buying a car. He agreed it was a "want" and not a "need," and he learned a lot by learning to cooperate with other family members.

I'm not suggesting that all families do this. What is important is the principle—don't do too much or make life easy for children. Let them make their own way. Allow them to solve their own problems. Sometimes we want to give our children all of the advantages we can—or we want them to be grateful to us—so we do too much.

Here are some typical problems children face that we might be tempted to solve.

- Jared is frustrated because he didn't get the class schedule he wanted.
- Ellen is hurt because a friend said something mean.
- Linda is unhappy she's not dating.
- Carlos finds it hard to do his homework.
- Devin got suspended for ditching school.
- Mike doesn't have money to go out with friends.

These are problems that children own. How often I've seen parents solve such problems for their children. They call the school to work out the class schedule. They sit every night to help Carlos with his homework. They try to arrange a date or convince Linda that she should not let not dating bother her. In short, we take on these problems as though they were our own and, by so doing, deprive our children of the opportunity to learn and grow. It reminds me of the well-meaning person who helps the butterfly emerge from the entrapment of its cocoon only to watch it die because it failed to develop the strength to fly.

This is not to say we can't be involved. We help children mature as we let them talk about their concerns and as we help them explore options and think through what they want to do. Yet it is important to remember where the ultimate responsibility resides. We don't own a problem simply because we're concerned. Being clear where responsibility ultimately lies is critical to a child's development.

## ASKING VALUING QUESTIONS

Asking Valuing Questions is the final responsibility skill. Although the last skill I'm discussing in this book, it is certainly not least in importance. In fact, the two skills I'm most likely to use during most problem-solving conversations with children, particularly teens, are listening and valuing. I start by listening. I want to be a safe place so my children can open up and tell me what they think and feel without fear that I'll take over the conversation or criticize or judge them. Listening not only builds trust and opens dialogue, but it also keeps responsibility where it ought to be—on my child. And by listening, we get to "bedrock," the solid ground of honest and real communication.

It is then that I shift my strategy to Asking Valuing Questions. "What will happen if this continues?" "Is that what you want?" "What do you want?" "What can you do to make that happen?" "What are the consequences if you do that?" And so on.

Questions and a willingness to listen evoke exploration, discovery, clarity, action, and commitment. They invite children and teens to look inside and think deeply about their lives, their values, and who they are becoming. Questions are powerful because they put our kids in the driver's seat and enable them to move beyond mere compliance (or rebellion) to live from personal strength and autonomy.

Loving parents desperately want their children to believe as they do, and so we are sometimes afraid of asking questions that might result in answers we don't want to hear. And yet, as we learn to ask questions rather than lecture and preach, we are in the process of building trust, goodwill, and closeness with our children and so increase our ability to influence them in positive ways.

Valuing is a structured process of asking questions that help children explore consequences, identify what they really want, and learn the actions necessary to bring it about. The skill is used when a child has a problem but needs help knowing how to deal with it.

Let me give you an example. Several years ago we had friends over on a Saturday evening. The kids were downstairs playing and adults upstairs visiting. I recall Melinda (probably six) coming upstairs crying. I called her over. "Come here, what's going on?"

"Jon hit me with the curtain rod."

"That didn't feel very good." I continued to hold her and empathize for a few minutes while she cried and told me how she was feeling. I then asked her a few questions. "What can you do?"

Her immediate response was, "Can you come down and get mad at Jon?"

"I guess I could, but it seems like this is between you and Jon. So, what can *you* do?" It took her a minute to get that I wasn't going to fix it for her. I said, "Let's think of every possible thing you could do and then you can choose."

She was quiet again.

"What are you thinking?" I asked.

She grinned. "I could go back down and hit Jon back."

"Oh, that would probably feel really good. And then what would happen?"

"He'd hit me again."

"Is that what you want?"

"No, I just want him to stop."

"Okay, so that's one choice. What else could you do?"

"I could go tell him to stop hitting me. I didn't like it."

"Yup. That's good. Anything else?"

She was a little stuck, so I primed the pump. "Some kids might go over to Katie's to see if she could play. Some little girls might go to their room to be alone… Can you think of anything else?"

"I could go start playing again."

Melinda jumped off my lap and was off. I don't know how she solved the problem. She figured something out.

This is an example in which I talked to Jon afterward. I didn't want to, at the moment, because I didn't want to take away Melinda's responsibility. But it isn't okay for a child to hit another. I invited Jon to tell me what happened. I listened but also let him know of my displeasure (disclosing skill), and then discussed some consequences if it happened again. As you can see, the valuing process teaches children to fish rather than giving them a fish. It is an alternative to lecturing, giving advice, or trying to solve their problems for them. Valuing places responsibility squarely on their shoulders to define what they want and how they'll make it happen. The skill consists of a set of questions that help children take control of their lives. Although there are many variations and ways of asking these questions, they follow a pattern:

1. **How do you feel about the way things (or _____) are going?** The answer may already be known or apparent from earlier in our conversation. If so, it's not necessary to ask this explicitly.

2. **What will happen if things keep going the way they are now?** This question invites children to take an honest look at the negative consequences of the situation and/or their behavior. They need to see consequences in order to change. We don't just ask this question once. We may follow up a first answer with, "What else?" or "Can you think of anything more?" We want them to get all their thoughts on the table.

3. **Is that what you want?** We help them explore this honestly. They need to see that what is happening is not what they want in the long

run. When asked to think honestly about what is happening, children begin to realize this trade-off.

4. **What do *you* want? Or, how would you like things to be?** This step invites children to begin to clarify their vision and what is most important to them—what is more important than what's happening now. Something has to be more important than what is happening now or they won't change.

5. **What can you do to accomplish this?** This is the heart of the process and places responsibility squarely on the shoulders of children. What are the specific actions you can take to get what you want? The initial reaction of many children, when faced with this question, is to blame or talk about what others could or should do. It is necessary to keep focusing on what the person seated in front of you can do. What do they have control over and not have control over?

6. **What problems or obstacles are you likely to encounter?** This is an opportunity to make their plan realistic. Explore the reality of problems they'll encounter and anticipate in advance how they will respond. It's one thing to come up with a plan, but carrying out that plan will, inevitably, be fraught by setbacks and hardships. We need to help kids anticipate these problems and work through them so they can find the courage and determination to change.

7. **What is your final commitment or plan?** This step calls for a final and concrete commitment. It should include the goal and actions to be taken as well as support the child may need from us or others. We can also set a time to get back together and review progress.

We don't always need to ask all of these questions when using valuing. Sometimes a single question, such as "What are the consequences if you do that?" "What options do you see?" or "What can you do to make that happen?" may be sufficient. The number of questions is not as critical as the fact that our children are encouraged to get in touch with their own inner resourcefulness and ability to choose.

During a valuing conversation, we often brainstorm by generating ideas and solutions together and then evaluating the possible results of each of those solutions. Upon further evaluation, some of the ideas may be rejected as impractical or unrealistic. Although both or all parties involved can be engaged in the process, it is important that most of the ideas come from the child who owns the problem and is seeking the solution. The process taps into the child's creativity and resourcefulness and helps him develop the confidence to manage his life effectively.

Let me share a few more examples of the skill. Mary (thirteen) and Beth (fifteen) are sisters who seem to bicker all the time. They wrangle as they do the dishes or other chores around the house. Mary complains that Beth takes her belongings without asking. Beth tells Mary to stop annoying her when she's on the phone. It goes on and on. The girls' mother decides to use valuing questions to talk to each of them. Here is her conversation with Beth.

Mother: "Beth, something that has been a concern to me lately is listening to you and Mary bicker with one another. I'm wondering if we could talk about it."

Beth: "There's really nothing to talk about. If anyone, you should be talking to Mary."

Mother: "Why do you say that?"

Beth: "She's so annoying. She's always trying to listen to my phone calls and makes faces at me and tries to bug me when I'm talking to friends."

Mother: "I've noticed that. What else bothers you?"

Notice that Mother wants to draw Beth out. She wants to start this conversation with empathy before going on to the valuing questions. Beth continues to complain about Mary, with Mother listening.

Mother: "Let me ask you something, Beth. What's going to happen if the two of you continue fighting as you have been lately?"

Beth: "Well, you should be talking to Mary. She's the one who starts it."

Mother: "No matter who starts it, do you like fighting with your sister?"

Beth: "I don't know. Not really, but I can't help it."

Mother: "What do you mean that you can't help it?" (A genuine question and not sarcasm.)

Beth: "I just get so mad that I want to make her shut up."

Mother listens, again, as Beth expresses her feelings. "Has your approach worked?"

Beth: "No."

Mother: "What do you think, is this going to get better or worse, considering how things are going?"

Beth: "Worse, I guess."

Mother: "Is that what you want?"

Beth: "Not really."

Mother: "What would you like in your relationship with your sister? How would you like things to be?"

Beth: "I'd just like some peace. I wish she'd leave me alone."

Mother: "I get that, Beth. This really is frustrating to you. So, let's think about some options here. What kinds of things could you do and say that might help her stop bugging you and leave you alone?"

Initially, Beth is a little resistant to this question. But her mother persists by asking such questions as: "Is it okay with you if it doesn't get better?" "What can you control and not control in your relationship with Mary?" "What might you be able to do or say that could help?" As her mother continues asking her questions, Beth starts to take some responsibility by talking about her own behaviors and not Mary's.

Mother: "Let's brainstorm. What might you be able to do or say so that Mary would be less likely to bug you?"

Beth: "I could tell her I really don't like it."

Mother: "How would you do that so she'd really be willing to listen and not ignore you?"

Beth is thoughtful for a moment. "I don't know. That's hard."

Mother is quiet.

Beth: "I suppose I'd need to start the talk in a friendly way."

Mother: "Good. How would you do that?"

Beth: "I'd go to her room and ask her how gymnastics is going. She'd probably like that."

Mother is quiet to let Beth continue thinking.

Beth: "Then I'd tell her I don't like how we've been fighting lately."

Mother: "How might she respond?"

The two talk it over with Mother coaching Beth by helping her continue to think through what she might say and how she might say it. They explore a few different scenarios until Beth is feeling more confident.

Mother: "This sounds really good, Beth. You're showing a lot of maturity by thinking about this. Let me ask you another question. Are you willing to be responsible for ways you bug Mary?"

Beth, feigning some surprise: "Like what?"

Mother: "Like borrowing her sweater without asking."

Beth is thoughtful. "You're right. I do some things that she doesn't like."

Mother: "Are you willing to let her know?"

Beth: "I guess so, if I want this to get better."

Mother: "Yeah. Be thinking about the kind of relationship you'd really like to have with your sister. You used to be really good friends."

Beth: "Thanks, Mom."


Of course, a conversation like this could go in different ways and, as parents, we need to flex to our children's responses. But be aware of the underlying principles involved. Good listening is often a foundational skill. Sometimes we make honesty statements. And, of course, the questions that this mother asks help Beth reflect more deeply and take responsibility for what's happening.

The shift may begin in one conversation. Sometimes it will take more, if trust is low and we have patterns of blame and arguing. But, if we persist, our children will hear the difference in our approach and start looking within instead of defending and arguing.

## VALUING WITH A GROUP

A number of years ago, my wife was director of a church play. The date was getting close, and she was concerned that the youth were not well prepared. One evening they were rehearsing at our house. The kids were energetic and rambunctious, not paying attention. Judy grew frustrated and finally stopped the rehearsal and had all the kids gather around. She asked them some questions.

Judy: "Whose responsibility is this road show?"

There were some snickers and whispers going around the room, so Judy did some disclosing. "I'm very disappointed tonight. It just seems like this is a big party or joke or something to you guys. As your leader, I feel very disrespected."

The room got very quiet.

"I'm hoping to have a good road show. But if I want a good road show and you guys don't care, then why am I doing this?" She was quiet, looking around the room. "So, how do you feel? Do you even want to be here? Because if not, then why should we pretend with each other?"

A teenage girl spoke up. "I want to be here. It's been fun and I'm really looking forward to it."

Judy: "Okay. Thank you. How about others?"

One young man spoke up. "I'm not excited about it. I'm embarrassed to sing and dance to these silly songs."

"Thank you for your honesty, Ben," said Judy. "Do others feel that way?"

After a moment, three or four hands went up.

"It's okay, you guys. I appreciate you being honest. How about others?"

A few other kids spoke up. "I like it." "It's cool." "We've come too far to not finish." "I think we've got a really good show."

Judy: "So let me ask you again. Who's responsible for this road show? Is it me?"

"No," came a chorus of voices.

"Who?"

"All of us," someone said.

"Who?" Judy asked again.

"All of us?"

"Who?"

"Me," came a reply from somewhere in the group.

"Who?"

Lots of "me's."

"Then what is it going to take to make this a good rehearsal?"

The youth started talking about some agreements. "We need to listen." "We have to pay attention and focus."

"Can we agree to do that, not only tonight but in the few rehearsals we have left?"

"Yes!" came a collective affirmation.

Judy looked at the guys who didn't want to be there. "How about you guys? I'm not going to force you to stay. It's your choice."

They all opted in.

Notice the principles again. Valuing is about placing responsibility where it ought to be. The key is asking questions that shift the responsibility from our shoulders to the shoulders of the youth. Doing so isn't that hard, but requires an understanding of the principle of responsibility. It takes practice. And, perhaps most of all, it takes believing in both the goodness and capability of our teenagers.

As we learn to ask the valuing questions, we empower others to look inside for answers rather than waiting for us to tell them how to think and feel or what to do. It is, indeed, a skill that will help them grow in responsibility and emotional maturity.

## SUMMARY

Our children are good and capable. The skills of Instilling Responsibility enable us to communicate with them in ways that help them uncover their potential and become self-governing, even at a young age.

## CREATING STRUCTURE

Children like and need structure and routine: meals, bedtime, chore charts, studying the Bible together

## ENFORCING CONSEQUENCES

- Establish few but fair rules (chores, respect, family time)
- Follow through with action (consequences) when expectations are violated
- Enforcement must be immediate, consistent, without guilt or hostility

## ENCOURAGING AUTONOMY

- Allow or give as many age-appropriate choices as possible
- Don't buy or do for them what they can do for themselves
- Allow them to struggle with life issues (be there/listen)

## ASKING VALUING QUESTIONS

- What do you think/feel about this?
- What are the consequences? Is that what you want?
- What do you want?
- What choices do you have?
- What can/will you do?
- How will you handle it if…?

# Final Thoughts

I ENJOYED WRITING THIS BOOK. Once I put my fingers on the keyboard, the words flowed quite easily. I realize how deeply I believe and trust these principles and skills. I hope they have resonated with you, my reader.

Of course, this doesn't mean that living the principles and skills is easy. There is little as dear to our hearts as our children, but also little that can cause so much heartache. Our children are not "objects" that can be readily understood or manipulated to do/be what we want. They come with predispositions, complex needs, emotions, and, of course, free will. Ultimately, they decide, not us. Therefore, there are no simple formulas. The work of parenting is as much art as science. It has more to do with the heart than the mind.

And yet, for the most part, we succeed as parents, not only because of what we do but because of what is inherent within our children. A seed planted in deep soil pushes upward (not downward or sideways) until it breaks out of the soil and into sunlight. Likewise, our children possess not only the physical, but spiritual DNA to succeed, to become who they are meant to be. We're along for the journey, witnesses to the process taking place.

My purpose has been to provide a framework, a set of principles and skills to make the parenting journey more understandable and pleasant. Let me offer a brief recap by returning to the principles–behavior–outcome model that describes the process of parenting.

| Principles ⟶ | Behavior ⟶ | Outcomes<br>A nurturing climate in which our children: |
|---|---|---|
| 1. We are the authority in our homes. | **Honesty Skills** | • Know of their goodness and worth |
| 2. Our children are inherently good, capable, and trustworthy. | • Disclosing<br>• Care-fronting<br>• Reproving | • Feel safe enough to talk |
| 3. Our children long to feel love and connection. | • Negotiating<br>• Harnessing | • Delay gratification and tolerate frustration |
| 4. We are responsible "to" but not "for" our children. | **Empathy Skills** | • Act rather than react |
| 5. Our children are responsible for themselves. | • Respecting<br>• Affirming<br>• Listening | • Solve problems and make good decisions<br>• Set and work toward goals |
| 6. Growth requires effort, even struggle. | • Supporting | • Make and keep commitments |
| 7. Limits and consequences teach wisdom and responsibility. | **Responsibility Skills**<br>• Creating structure | • Act from a moral and spiritual compass<br>• Respect and cooperate with others |
| 8. Successful parenting requires that we grow ourselves first. | • Enforcing consequences<br>• Encouraging autonomy | |
| 9. We're imperfect (and that's okay). | • Valuing | |

Good parenting is grounded in sound principles. Like a rudder on a ship, principles guide us, help us stay on course, inform us of behaviors that are strengthening rather than weakening. Without principles, we are much more likely to react and fall into the weakening tendencies of over managing and overindulging. Therefore, I encourage you to think deeply about these principles. As we ponder and internalize them, our actions will change. Correct principles lead to good, healthy communication and behavior. If we want to change our parenting behavior, we need to first become grounded in sound principles.

The outcomes listed in the chart above are the ideal. This is what most of us desire within our homes and families. Of course, there is always a difference between the ideal and the real. Even the best families fall short. That is okay as long as we keep a standard in mind. As I stated elsewhere, our goal is progress, not perfection.

The HERO principle will guide us in how to parent on a day-to-day basis.

**H**onesty + **E**mpathy + **R**esponsibility = **O**utcomes

Honesty, empathy, and responsibility are behaviors, specific communication techniques that lead to positive outcomes. The skills associated with each are alternatives to over managing and overindulging. For most of us, these skills don't come naturally. We have to practice them. And like learning any new skill (playing an instrument, speaking a language, sewing, cooking, dribbling a ball), we get better with practice. The good news is that our children give us lots of opportunities to practice. Come to think of it, we get to practice every time we face a new key moment. Perhaps we should be more thankful for our key moments.

I want to conclude with one of my favorite quotes. It's from *The Inner Game of Tennis*, a book by W. Timothy Gallwey.

*When we plant a rose seed in the earth we notice that it is small but we do not criticize it as rootless and stem less. We treat it as a seed, giving it the water and nourishment required of a seed. When it first shoots up out of the earth, we don't condemn it as immature and underdeveloped; nor do we criticize the buds for not being open when they appear. We stand in wonder at the process taking place and give the plant the care it needs at each stage of its development. The rose is a rose from the time it is a seed until the time it dies. Within it, at all times, it contains its whole potential. It seems to be constantly in the process of change; yet at each stage, at each moment, it is perfectly alright as it is.*

Our children are imperfect creatures, immature and underdeveloped in so many ways. May we learn to be less judgmental and stand in wonder at what is taking place before our eyes. May we trust this process, believing in the potential that is so often not before our eyes.

And let's do the same with ourselves. We, too, are imperfect in this journey. Let's opt to be gentle and easy with ourselves and give ourselves the care we need at each stage of our journey. Like our children, we, too, are growing. Yet within us are the seeds of incredible potential which will blossom as we *choose* the principles and behaviors by which we want to parent.

Thank you for allowing me to be part of your journey.

# Appendix

# A Quick Guide to Principles of Raising Responsible, Emotionally Mature Children

❖ ❖ ❖

PARENTING IS NOT ABOUT GET-
TING our children to do what we want, which often leads to over managing or overindulging them. It is about creating loving relationships and a nurturing home which enable

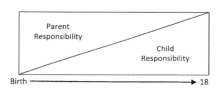

them to feel good about themselves, develop a sense of who they are, and learn to solve problems and take full responsibility for their decisions. (**We are gardeners not mechanics.**)

## THREE STYLES OF PARENTING:

**Permissive parenting**—Absence of structure, discipline, or routine. Parents may feel lots of love but fail to trust their own authority and so give too much power and control to kids. Do too much for their kids. Avoid conflict. Try to make sure kids are happy. Kids become entitled with inflated expectations of themselves and what life owes them.

**Authoritarian parenting**—Lots of structure and rules. Parents are in charge. They are insecure about their children's ability to make choices, so they over control (drill sergeant) and/or overprotect (helicopter). Children do not develop responsibility for self or emotional maturity. They learn to listen to outside voices and so become compliant (good child) or rebel (bad child).

**Nurturing parenting**—Lots of love and respect between family members. Children are seen as inherently good, worthy, and capable. Parents trust their own authority and use it to set boundaries and create a positive environment rather than control. They support their children in their challenges and decisions, knowing where the responsibility ultimately lies, and allowing their children to make their own decisions and solve their own problems.

## PRINCIPLES OF A NURTURING HOME:

1. **We, as parents, are the authority in our homes.** Due to our knowledge, capability, and experience, we have a duty to preside. We must be strong enough to establish our authority and use this authority to create a positive, nurturing environment with clear expectations, routines, traditions, and loving communication. We are firm and fair. We say what we mean and mean what we say.

2. **Our children are inherently good, capable, and trustworthy.** We make it easier for our children if we believe in them. Positive assumptions allow us to communicate and act from respect and trust (rather than fear and mistrust), which enables children to build self-worth, gain confidence, and make good choices.

3. **Our children long to feel love and connection.** There is no better way to inoculate our children from the storms of life than being emotionally safe, sensitive, and responsive to their needs and inner experience. There is no better way to help them feel good about themselves than offering our non-possessive care and attention. Of course, we can offer. They have to choose to accept our love.

4. **We are responsible "to" but not "for" our children.** It is easy to overstep boundaries and rob our children of their agency. We set expectations, teach, and then support our children in their challenges by allowing them to carry out their own responsibilities, solve their own problems, and make their own decisions. By trying

to do this for them, we steal from them growth opportunities of great value.

| If I feel *responsible for* my children, I... | If I feel *responsible to* my children, I... |
|---|---|
| • Fix, solve, protect, rescue, and control | • Listen, encourage, support, love |
| • Feel tired, worried, fearful, unappreciated | • Feel relaxed, trusting, confident, appreciated |
| • Expect them to live up to my expectations | • Trust them to live up to their own expectations |
| • Manipulate them to make sure things turn out right | • Am concerned with enjoying our relationship |

5. **Our children are responsible for themselves.** We cannot control our children and make them think, feel, and do exactly as we want. We may lecture, preach, threaten, and nag our kids to do their homework, choose good friends, etc., but we cannot follow them around and ensure that they do as we wish. They own their lives and have to learn to make their own choices.

6. **Growth requires effort, even struggle.** It is easy to over-parent our children by hovering, rescuing, and doing too much or expecting too little of them. Doing so creates entitlement as our children learn lessons that are inconsistent with the realities of life. Home life should not be a free ride. We should not feel guilty about letting our children struggle to learn the lessons of life.

7. **Limits and consequences teach wisdom and responsibility.** Reality, experience, and consequences are the most powerful teacher of life's lessons. Don't hold a job, can't buy a car. Don't come to dinner when called, go hungry. Forget an assignment, get marked down. Our children learn wisdom and responsibility through consequences (not preaching, threatening, and nagging). Act more and talk less.

8. **Parenting requires that we grow ourselves first.** The biggest challenge to parenting is not our children's behavior but our own emotional reactivity. When reactive, we regress to immature words and actions, causing our children to be defensive and self-protective so

they fail to learn from their mistakes. Loving parenting is not about getting our children to be different as much as getting ourselves to be different. Children want parents who are calm yet firm.

9. **We are imperfect (and that is okay).** As we accept our imperfections, we become more real. We allow our children to have their imperfections and feel our love and forgiveness so they can talk, explore, "own," and work through their mistakes.

# The HERO Principle of Parenting:

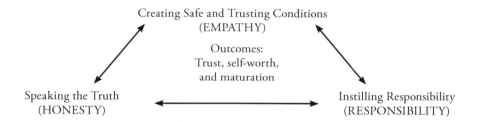

Creating Safe and Trusting Conditions
(EMPATHY)

Outcomes:
Trust, self-worth,
and maturation

Speaking the Truth
(HONESTY)

Instilling Responsibility
(RESPONSIBILITY)

| HONESTY SKILLS | EMPATHY SKILLS | RESPONSIBILITY SKILLS |
|---|---|---|
| **Disclosing**-This is what is important to me... This is what I believe and why... What do you think?<br><br>**Care-fronting:** This is what I see happening... Here are the consequences I see...<br><br>**Reproving**<br>1. Give clear (even sharp) correction<br>2. Ask (or tell) next step<br>3. Disengage<br>4. If failure to comply, impose consequence<br><br>**Negotiating Agreements**<br>1. Develop a common understanding of perceptions/feelings of each person<br>2. Discover what is important to each person<br>3. Brainstorm possible solutions<br>4. Agree upon solutions that meet the needs of all parties<br><br>**Harnessing Harmful Behavior**<br>1. Initiate conversation<br>2. Invite child to share point of view<br>3. Place responsibility with questions<br>4. Process faulty thinking (victim, blame, etc.)<br>5. Jointly create a plan<br>6. Determine reward | **Respecting**-Seeing goodness and uniqueness<br>• Allow them to be who they are<br>• Join them in their world<br>• Take time<br>• Honor their boundaries<br><br>**Affirming**-Communicating love and goodwill<br>• Acknowledge a quality of being<br>• Touch, hug, smile (nonverbal love)<br>• Tell them you love them<br><br>**Listening**-Suspending judgment and tendency to react; be present to understand child's experience/point of view<br>• Tell me more...<br>• So you feel...<br>• Let me see if I understand...<br><br>**Supporting**-Asking, rather than guessing or taking over<br>• What do you need?<br>• How can I support you? | **Creating Structure**-Children like and need structure and routine: meals, bedtime, chore charts, family prayer<br><br>**Enforcing Consequences**<br>• Establish few but fair rules (chores, respect, family time)<br>• Follow through with action (consequences) when expectation violated<br>• Enforcement must be immediate, consistent, without guilt or hostility<br><br>**Encouraging Autonomy**<br>• Give age-appropriate choices<br>• Don't buy or do for them what they can do for self<br>• Allow them to struggle with life issues (be there/listen)<br><br>**Asking Valuing Questions**<br>• What do you think/feel about this?<br>• What are the consequences? Is that what you want?<br>• What do you want?<br>• What choices do you have?<br>• What can/will you do?<br>• How will you handle it if...? |

# Recommended Parenting Books

Allen, C. Kay. *Journey from Fear to Love: 6 Concepts and Skills That Will Change Your Life.* Denver, Human Values Institute, 1980

Cline, Foster and Fay, Jim. *Parenting Teens with Love and Logic: Preparing Adolescents for Responsible Adulthood.* Colorado Springs, Pinon Press, 1992

Dinkmeyer, Don and McKay, Gary. *Raising a Responsible Child: Practical Steps to Successful Family Relationships.* New York, Simon & Schuster, 1973

Dreikurs, Rodulf and Soltz, Vicki. *Children: The Challenge.* New York, Hawthorne, 1964

Faber, Adele and Mazlish, Elaine. *How to Talk so Kids Will Listen and Listen so Kids Will Talk.* Saddle Brook, NJ, American Book-Stratford Press, 1980

Fay, Jim and Fay, Charles. *Love and Logic Magic for Early Childhood: Practical Parenting from Birth to Six Years.* Golden, CO, Love and Logic Press, 2000

Ginott, Haim. *Between Parent and Child.* New York, Avon, 1969

Goddard, H. Wallace. *Bringing up Children in Light and Truth.* Brigham City, UT, Currawong Press, 2013

Gordon, Thomas. Parenting *Effectiveness Training: The Tested New Way to Raise Responsible Children.* New York, Plume, 1970

Gottman, John. *Raising an Emotionally Intelligent Child: The Heart of Parenting.* New York, Simon & Schuster, 2011

Latham, Glenn, I. *The Power of Positive Parenting: A Wonderful Way to Raise Children.* Logan, UT, Parenting Prescriptions, 2012

# The Key Moment Model

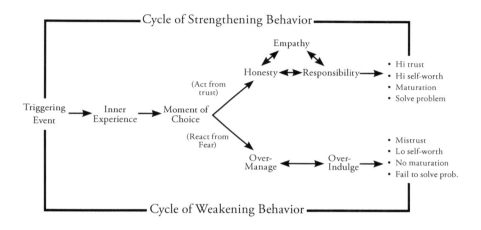

# Weakening Behaviors

MANY NATURAL RESPONSES, WHEN FACING a challenge (key moment), are weakening. They impose control from without rather than building responsibility and self-discipline from within. They rob children of their ability to be self-governing and cause them to be externally driven. We do this in two ways:

**Over Controlling**

**Lecturing:** Moralizing and telling children how to think, feel, and act, which builds resentment and deprives them of the opportunity to think for themselves.

**Arguing:** Getting caught up in verbal battles, trying to convince each other that we're "right" and they are "wrong," which only leads to more entrenched positions.

**Criticizing:** Finding fault and making negative comments about their character or behavior to try to get them to do what we want.

**Getting Mad:** Yelling, hitting, fuming, etc. Expresses parent's powerlessness and causes the child to feel resentment and shame.

**Giving Advice ("nifty plans"):** Telling kids what to do or how to solve their problems. It will usually be rejected. Even if accepted, it breeds dependency and lack of faith in self.

**Comparing:** Pointing out differences between one child and another to either make him feel good or get him to change.

**Blaming:** Accusing another of negative motives or attributing a negative situation to her.

**Threatening:** Verbally expressing an intention to impose a severe consequence on a child, often with no intent to carry it out.

**Nagging:** Constantly scolding, reminding, or complaining to get a child to do what you want.

# Weakening Behaviors

## Overindulging

**Hovering:** Being overly aware and responsive to a child's every move. Failure to allow her the physical or emotional space to make choices or act on her own.

**Sympathizing:** Communicating pity for what a child is going through. Different from empathy. Rewards him for feeling bad rather than taking action.

**Avoiding:** Withdrawing into ourselves and leaving our children without support, structure, or guidance because we are uncertain or overwhelmed by their needs.

**Catering:** Giving in to a child's whims and wishes. Bending over backward to keep him happy or making sure that things go his way so he won't be upset.

**Fixing:** Solving a problem or doing for a child what she could and should be able to do for herself—making a bed, choosing clothes, talking to a teacher.

**Rescuing:** Trying to make a child feel better by undoing consequences or not allowing a child to face the consequences of his actions or choices.

**Protecting:** Preventing a child from facing the realities of life by not letting her engage in experiences that involve social, emotional, or even physical risk.

**Flip-flopping:** Setting a boundary and then renegotiating because it was not convenient, the kids pushed back, or you thought you were being harsh.

**Pleading:** Begging kids to do what you want rather than expecting and letting them be responsible.

**Bribing:** Making a promise to do something or give the child something to get him to do what you want, something he should probably be doing anyway.

**Giving in:** Wearing down as you hear whining or complaints. Letting a child do/have what she wants to avoid enforcing a boundary. It is easier.

# Key Moment Exercise

1. **Event**
   a. What happened?

   b. What, specifically, about the event triggered your reaction?

2. **Thoughts**
   a. How did you interpret the event?

   b. What negative thoughts about your children or the event caused you to react?

3. **Feelings**
   a. What physical sensations did you experience?

   b. What emotions did you feel?

4. **Behavior**
   a. What did you do during the key moment?

   b. What did you do afterwards?

5. **Consequences**
   a. What were the immediate consequences of how you reacted?

   b. What are the long-term consequences?

6. As you look back, how are you feeling about how you handled this key moment?

7. What might you do differently in the future?

# Earnings Chart

| Behavior | Possible points | Mon | Tue | Wed | Thu | Fri | Sat | Sun |
|---|---|---|---|---|---|---|---|---|
| In room till 7:00 | 20 | 0 | 20 | 20 | 0 | 20 | 0 | 20 |
| Ready for day before breakfast (dressed, hair, bed) | 20 | 20 | 20 | 20 | 20 | 20 | 20 | 20 |
| Morning chores | 20 | 0 | 0 | 20 | 20 | 0 | 20 | 20 |
| Enrichment (math, writing) | 20 | 20 | 20 | 0 | 20 | 20 | * | * |
| Pack lunch | 10 | 10 | 10 | 0 | 10 | 10 | * | * |
| Respectful and cooperative | 30 | 0 | 30 | 0 | 30 | 30 | 0 | 30 |
| Good with babies | 10 | 10 | 10 | 0 | 10 | 10 | 0 | 10 |
| Complete homework or good quiet time | 20 | 20 | 20 | 0 | 20 | 20 | 20 | 20 |
| Feed dog by 5:00 | 10 | 10 | 10 | 0 | 10 | 10 | 0 | 10 |
| Set table | 20 | 20 | 20 | 20 | 0 | 20 | 0 | 20 |
| Bed on time | 20 | 0 | 20 | 20 | 0 | 0 | 20 | 20 |
| | | | | | | | | |
| | | | | | | | | |
| Total | 200 | 110 | 180 | 100 | 140 | 160 | 110 | 200 |

*Points count, although don't need to do these behaviors on these days

**Daily Rewards**

200: Stay up till 9:00 p.m., snack; special activity (Wii, game, short movie)

170–190: Stay up until 8:30; snack; extra book

150–170: Snack and book

120–150: Bedtime snack

Below 120: Bed at 8:00

**Weekly Rewards**

- Points convert to money.
- If _____ earns 800 points by Friday evening, she can plan a date with Mom or Dad for weekend.

Signed: _____ Date: _____

# About the Author

ROGER K. ALLEN, PH.D., is an expert in personal development and family relationships as well as organizational leadership and teams. Using his engaging style, Roger has delivered hundreds of workshops, retreats, and seminars around the country which have been acclaimed as among the most powerful learning experiences available anywhere.

Beginning in 1980, Roger founded and served as president of the Human Development Institute, providing thousands of hours of individual, marriage, and family therapy to a diverse client population and supervising the work of other members of the professional staff. During this time he created and taught, along with other HDI staff, experiential programs in personal development and family relations in a number of cities around the country.

In 1992, Roger, along with Preston Pond, co-founded the Center for Organizational Design to help leaders create high performance organizations. Roger helps leaders do the deep work to become a cohesive team capable of defining the direction of the organization and rallying employees behind them to achieve outstanding and sustainable business results. He has spearheaded major executive and organizational development projects with many Fortune 500 companies.

Programs developed by Roger have helped hundreds of organizations and hundreds of thousands of people transform their personal and professional lives. More than 800 trainers, coaches, and consultants from around the country have been certified to teach programs that Roger and his business partners have developed.

An outdoor enthusiast and father of four adult children and fifteen grandchildren, Roger resides in metro Denver, Colorado, with his wife Judy.

To learn more about Roger Allen and raising responsible, emotionally mature children, visit:

www.raisingresponsiblechildren.com
www.rogerkallen.com
or email
info@rogerkallen.com

Made in the USA
San Bernardino, CA
17 February 2020

64570381R00098